Counselling and Psychotherapy in Contemporary Private Practice

Edited by Adrian Hemmings and Rosalind Field

 Routledge
Taylor & Francis Group

LONDON AND NEW YORK

First published 2007 by Routledge
27 Church Road, Hove, East Sussex BN3 2FA

Simultaneously published in the USA and Canada
by Routledge
270 Madison Avenue, New York, NY 10016

Routledge is an imprint of the Taylor & Francis Group, an Informa business

Typeset in Sabon by Garfield Morgan, Swansea, West Glamorgan
Printed and bound in Great Britain by TJ International Ltd, Padstow,
Cornwall
Paperback cover design by Lisa Dynan

This publication has been produced with paper manufactured to strict
environmental standards and with pulp derived from sustainable forests.

British Library Cataloguing in Publication Data
A catalogue record for this book is available from the British Library

Library of Congress Cataloging in Publication Data
Counselling and psychotherapy in contemporary private practice / edited
by Adrian Hemmings & Rosalind Field.
     p. cm.
   Includes bibliographical references.
   ISBN 978-1-58391-245-4 (hardback) – ISBN 978-1-58391-246-1 (pbk.)
1. Counseling psychology–Practice. 2. Counseling psychology–Moral and
ethical aspects. 3. Psychotherapy–Practice. 4. Psychotherapy–Moral and
ethical aspects. I. Hemmings, Adrian, 1952- II. Field, Rosalind, 1961-
   BF636.6.C675 2007
   158'.3–dc22

                                                           2007004671

ISBN 978-1-58391-245-4 (hbk)
ISBN 978-1-58391-246-1 (pbk)

Contents

Contributors

Jeremy Christey has worked in the therapy field for over 20 years, in a number of areas including HIV, drugs, young people and extensively in the NHS. He specializes in working with underlying dynamic issues in a cognitive behavioural and conversational framework. He works in Brighton and the surrounding areas with his company, Talking Therapies Ltd, renovating houses and skippering a racing yacht in his spare time.

Rosalind Field UKCP has had a private practice in Brighton since 1987. Rosalind has an MSc in social work and has had many years' experience working with children and families in Family Therapy and Family Mediation, both for various social service departments and voluntary sector organizations. Rosalind is also a qualified and experienced psychotherapy supervisor.

Andrea Halewood is a Chartered Counselling Psychologist in private practice and a lecturer in Counselling Psychology at Roehampton University. She has worked as a practice counsellor in Primary Care for South London and Maudsley NHS Trust and as a research psychologist for the Fetal Medicine Foundation investigating patient comprehension of numerical risk.

Adrian Hemmings is a chartered psychologist and senior practitioner on the British Psychological Society (BPS) Register of Psychologists Specialising in Psychotherapy. Adrian currently works in the NHS as a psychologist and psychotherapist in a local Primary Care Trust where he is Professional Head of Psychology. He trained as a psychotherapist and has worked in private practice for 20 years.

Dr Glyn Hudson-Allez is a BPS Chartered Psychologist, specializing in Counselling and Forensic issues, and is a UKCP Registered Psychosexual Therapist. She has worked as a counsellor for 25 years, eight of which were in primary health care. She currently has a large private practice. She has published numerous papers, theses and book chapters, and two books: *Time Limited Therapy in a General Practice Setting* (1997, Sage) and *Sex and Sexuality: Questions and Answers for Counsellors and Psychotherapists* (2005, Whurr). She is currently writing her third book about neuroscience and attachments. Glyn has a lifetime fellowship from the Association of Counsellors and Psychotherapists in Primary Care (CPC), and is former Training Manager for the British Association for Sexual and Relationship Therapy (BASRT).

Lawrence Suss is a senior registered member of BACP, a UKCP registered psychoanalytic psychotherapist and supervisor, and is a Professional member and former chair of the Association for Group and Individual Psychotherapy. He is a part-time senior lecturer in counselling at the University of Brighton where he is course leader of the Postgraduate Diploma in Psychodynamic Counselling. He has a busy counselling and psychotherapy practice in Brighton.

Melanie Withers originally read English at Bristol University. A qualified teacher, she worked in further education as a lecturer for ten years. She trained as a counsellor and supervisor at Brighton and Sussex Universities. She is co-founder and Clinical Director of the Rock Clinic Association in Brighton where she works in private practice as a counsellor, supervisor and consultant. She is currently Director of the Counselling Unit at the University of Sussex and a Senior Accredited Member of BACP.

Robert Withers trained to be a homeopath, then an acupuncturist after completing a degree in philosophy. He went on to research homeopathy academically and finally trained to be a psychotherapist and Jungian analyst. Throughout this time he has maintained a busy private practice, initially as a complementary therapist and then as an analyst and supervisor of counsellors and therapists. He is in addition a senior lecturer in the School of Integrated Health at the University of Westminster and visiting lecturer at the Inter-university College, Graz. His publications include editor and contributor to *Controversies in Analytical Psychology* (2003, Brunner-Routledge) and 'Psychoanalysis Complementary Medicine and the Placebo' in D. Peters (ed.) *Understanding the Placebo Effect in Complementary Medicine* (2001, Churchill Livingstone).

Chapter 1

Introduction

Rosalind Field and Adrian Hemmings

Up until the mid-1990s starting an independent practice was a comparatively uncomplicated undertaking. It was not unusual to complete a counselling or psychotherapy training and immediately set up in independent practice. Currently, however, with the gradual professionalization of counselling and psychotherapy there are an increasing number of jobs available in the voluntary sector as well as within the NHS. These may be either salaried or unpaid positions, and practitioners may prefer to gain experience within the potentially more supportive environment of an organization before setting up on their own. Indeed, many counselling and psychotherapy training organizations insist that their graduates do not set up in independent practice until they have gained considerable experience working within one of these organizations. The British Association of Counselling and Psychotherapy (BACP) suggests that 'ideally, a counsellor in independent practice should have substantial training and experience'. Therefore this book is as much for experienced practitioners of counselling and psychotherapy as it is for trainee and newly qualified therapists contemplating setting up as an independent practitioner in the future.

The future role of the independent counsellor or psychotherapist is particularly pertinent in a period of NHS deficits, financial cuts and the world of financial 'turnaround teams'. Currently, there appears to be a shift in the focus of primary care counselling from clients with mild to moderate difficulties to those with moderate to severe. This means that patients with mild to moderate difficulties and those who do not fit into an obvious diagnostic category are likely to fall through the net and may be told by their GP to seek independent counselling practitioners or psychotherapists. This could have a profound effect on contemporary independent practice.

While this book does offer some practical ideas, this is not its main focus. There are several books of this kind already on the market (McMahon 1994; Syme 1994; Thistle 1998; Clarke 2002; Feltham and Horton 2006). Instead we present the reader with issues that arise from the specific context of working in independent practice and explore how these affect what takes place in the therapeutic relationship.

The contributors to the book are all experienced practitioners who work or have worked independently as well as within the public sector. They have drawn on their own experience to illustrate their ideas and to engage the reader in thinking creatively about the issues. While most of the contributors use a psychodynamic paradigm with which to illustrate their ideas, the issues examined are highly relevant to practitioners using other theoretical models.

Counselling is a relatively new profession and as such is developing its identity. In the light of this Dr Glyn Hudson-Allez sets the scene of the book with her chapter on the history of counselling in independent practice. She describes the increasing availability of paid positions for counsellors in primary care and explores the impact of this on the independent practitioner. She moves on to discuss current developments in counselling in general such as practice-based commissioning (PBC) and in independent practice specifically.

Chapter 3 by Lawrence Suss introduces the thorny question of where one finds clients once we have decided to set up in independent practice. Until recently, advertising was frowned upon by many professions including medicine and the allied professions such as counselling and psychotherapy. In the last decade there has been a radical change in the culture that, combined with recent advances in information technology, has made advertising not only possible but almost a necessity. The topics covered in this chapter range from the ethics to the merits of advertising. Different forms of advertising are discussed from a simple leaflet to more complex media such as Yellow Pages and the internet. Advertising affects client expectations of counselling and the impact of this on practice is also explored.

Once we have attracted our client, how do we progress when we have none of the usual procedures imposed by working in an organization? Chapter 4 by Melanie Withers on assessment addresses this. While she highlights the need for assessment, she also introduces the notion that in independent practice the client has purchasing power. He or she may shop around for the therapist that suits them and therefore has more choice. Assessment becomes a two-way process.

In Chapter 5 on working with other professionals, Adrian Hemmings explores the issue of working with the background presence of GPs, social workers and other practitioners, and the dangers of splitting both by the client and the professionals concerned. He also discusses the concept of the 'other's' presence in the therapeutic work where there is no direct contact between the 'other' and the therapist. While the term 'other' mainly refers to other professionals, it may also fall into the category of a substance such as a drug (therapeutic or illegal). The 'other' may also be a 'significant other', that is, a family member who is metaphorically brought into the room by the client but who nevertheless has an impact on the work. The subsequent chapters move on to examine the issues that arise when working within specific environments.

In choosing to work in independent practice counsellors and psychotherapists are faced with the decision of whether to work from home or whether to rent a consulting room in a clinic. Some clinics are run along the lines of a group counselling practice offering practitioners a dedicated environment in which to set up their work. In Chapter 6 Jeremy Christey and Andrea Halewood describe how, by choosing to work in a group practice, the independent therapist steps into the world of organizational dynamics. Using Bion's theory of 'basic assumptions', they explore the issues involved in working within this context. Using examples from their own experience they explore the dynamics within the team of practitioners that can be mirrored in the work with their clients to positive or negative effect.

Increasingly practitioners choose to work in a complementary health clinic where the environment is not dedicated specifically to counselling or psychotherapy. Robert Withers is a Jungian analyst but also trained and worked as a homeopath and an acupuncturist. In Chapter 7 he examines the dynamics of working with other complementary health workers. He discusses the notion of professional territoriality, confounding the assumption that complementary health suggests a group of practitioners who are willing to collaborate with other practitioners in an integrated health care setting. Difficult obstacles are presented to the practitioner working in this context such as competition in the marketplace, professional rivalry and differing and conflicting models of symptom causation and cure. The danger of being invited into a mind/body split is particularly potent when working in this environment.

In Chapter 8 Rosalind Field discusses the advantages and disadvantages when the practitioner opts to work from home. She explores the notion that working in this context creates specific boundary issues that affect both the therapeutic work and other family members who share the therapist's home. She makes particular reference to how envy plays a part in these relationships and explores the dilemmas that this creates. Using composite clinical vignettes, she describes her own attempts to address this.

Peculiar to working independently the practitioner is confronted with the matter of money. The way in which client and therapist relate to money and how this may be played out in the work are areas discussed in Chapter 9 by Adrian Hemmings and Rosalind Field. They also examine the significance of the way in which the client actually pays the therapist and how this might offer information to the therapist as to what is happening within the therapeutic relationship. Also explored is the fact that the act of payment becomes part of the therapeutic frame setting.

Fittingly, the final chapter of the book by Rosalind Field is on endings. Inevitably the therapeutic relationship comes to an end, whatever the working context. However, Chapter 10 examines the nature of ending itself and how this may create particular tensions if working in independent practice. One such tension is the potential for fiscal dependence by the therapist on the client. This may affect the therapist's professional judgement as to whether or not it is appropriate for the client to leave the therapy. She introduces the idea of 'forced endings', particularly focusing on the situation where the therapist becomes pregnant. When this occurs the therapist's personal needs interrupt the therapeutic frame. However, this powerful metaphor creates profound dynamics of its own. Other situations such as taking holidays, therapist's illness and the necessity for interim cover are also examined in this chapter.

The issues discussed in this book are those that have emerged from the authors' own experiences and they propose a series of dilemmas for which they do not purport to have the answers. Where they give examples, they endeavour to describe how they have handled each situation, and in doing this invite the reader to become mindful of these issues and to accommodate the paradoxes that may arise.

References

Clarke, J. (2002) *Freelance Counselling and Psychotherapy: Competition and Collaboration*, Hove: Brunner-Routledge.

Feltham, C. and Horton, I. (2006) *The Sage Handbook of Counselling and Psychotherapy*, 2nd edn, London: Sage.

McMahon, G. (1994) *Setting Up Your Own Private Practice in Counselling and Psychotherapy*, Cambridge: NEC.

Syme, G. (1994) *Counselling in Independent Practice*, Maidenhead: Open University Press.

Thistle, R. (1998) *Counselling and Psychotherapy in Private Practice: Professional Skills for Counsellors*, London: Sage.

Chapter 2

The changing status of counselling and its impact on private practice

Glyn Hudson-Allez

Introduction

When I first undertook training as a counsellor in the early 1980s, counselling in the UK was very different from what it is today. A new way of thinking about counselling and psychotherapy was emerging at that time. There were few formal courses. Most therapists learning their skills through reading, dialogue with peers, seminars or being members of analytical societies. The British Association for Counselling (now BACP) was a small interest group. There was no United Kingdom Council for Psychotherapy (UKCP), no British Confederation of Psychotherapists (BCP) no Counsellors and Psychotherapists in Primary Care (CPC). While there was a special interest group in psychotherapy, the counselling division of the British Psychological Society (BPS) did not exist, nor did appropriate guidelines or codes of ethics. The whole concept of psychotherapy was considered rather alternative and typically American, and was regarded sceptically by the medical profession. Many private therapists worked on a basis of a preferred theoretical model with no formal qualifications as there were few awarding bodies to provide them.

The Foster Report of 1971 was the first published government initiative toward regulating the profession and restricting its implementation only to those who had appropriate training. This chapter will focus on the emerging profession of counselling and psychotherapy since that time, and discuss how that transformation now affects counsellors and psychotherapists who work in private practice. I will use the term 'therapist' as a generic term to apply to any counsellor, psychologist or psychotherapist working in a clinical setting providing therapy. I will also use the terms 'patient' for users of the NHS system and 'client' for those attending a private practitioner.

The move towards regulation

Regulation of the profession is not a new idea. It has been ubiquitously discussed in various reports over the last 30 years. As already mentioned, it started with the Foster Report as a consequence of fears about the rapid spread of Scientology, and was followed by the Seighart Report in 1978, which proposed the establishment of a Psychotherapy Council. However, the government of the day was of a mind to let the psychotherapists regulate themselves. Three years after this report, a Private Member's Bill to regulate psychotherapy and counselling failed in its second reading and it was this that led to the opportunity of establishing the UKCP. The subsequent development of moves to self-regulate in order to protect both the public and the profession by means of professional registers swung into place. Further attempts to regulate psychotherapy came with a Private Member's Bill proposed by Lord Alderdice in 2000–2002, but again did not make it past the Committee stage in the Lords. The government per se has been reluctant to become involved in the process when there is such a division with the professions of counselling, psychotherapy and psychoanalysis as to appropriate standards on qualifications, training and professional standards. These peaks and troughs in attempts to regulate the profession have probably provided the most influential swing of change, whilst at the same time being the most fiercely debated process of development to the current form of counselling used by the private practitioner (Mowbray 1995; Baron 1996; Frankland 1997).

Regulation per se brings together groups of therapists to form cohesive groups that metamorphose into professional bodies. These organizations position themselves between the membership and the state, providing a professional identity for the former, and recognition and legitimacy in its dealings with the latter, whose aim is to protect the user. The USA, as always, was ahead of the UK on this. They already have statutory regulation by means of a licence, which is only issued if certain qualifications are met. It also regulates the use of the title of 'psychotherapist', thus prohibiting anyone using the title unless they have got the appropriate qualifications and licence. However, the US regulatory licences are not without their critics, particularly with the problems of being portable between one state and another. The UK may experience similar difficulties if Scotland, Wales, Northern Ireland and England all choose to adopt their own methods of credentialing.

Movement into primary care settings

The next big change within the profession came as pressure was applied from those involved in preventative healthcare to move counselling and psychotherapy into medical contexts to work alongside medical professionals. Again this was following the initiative in the United States, but there the defining factor of any psychotherapeutic help offered to patients was financial, not clinical. Health maintenance organizations (HMOs), developed by the health insurance industry, have been progressively withdrawing the funding of psychotherapeutic interventions that are not evidence based and refuse to employ counsellors or psychotherapists who have no formal qualifications. What happens in the USA tends to follow on in the UK within five years or so. In the UK the move started in the early 1980s and was reinforced when the Counselling in Medical Settings section of the BACP (now FHPC) was established in 1985.

By the time I published my first paper on the issue in 1988, counselling within primary care was emerging, but still a minority occupation (Hudson 1988), and still meeting with a lot of resistance from health authorities. The medical profession, interestingly though, was becoming much more open to introducing counsellors into primary care, as a result of a psychotherapist who ran GP work groups (Balint 1974). GPs started using innovative methods to sidestep family practitioner rules for employing non-medical staff by using the ancillary staff budget as a means to bring therapists into the practice. However, once GPs were given their own fundholding budget, there was a positive mushrooming of therapists moving into primary care settings, until today it is considered that 81 per cent of GP surgeries now have access to a primary care counselling service (Wilkin et al. 1999).

Of course, this is not happening in every area throughout the UK. Some counties are providing a comprehensive primary care counselling service with a therapist in every GP practice, while in other areas there is no service at all. Thus the much-heralded government concept of removing fundholding from GPs in order to provide equity of provision throughout the country has not resulted in this aim being achieved as yet. Counselling in primary care is still a benefit of postal code, but the expansion in primary care has had a ripple effect on to employment assistance programmes (EAPs) and private practice as the public demand for talking cures increases. Thus, there is a direct correlation between access to NHS-supported counselling and the growth demand for counselling in the private sector.

Practice-based commissioning

Practice-based commissioning (PBC) is a recent government initiative whereby GP practices or groups of practices can commission services that are not part of the NHS but part of non-profit making independent organizations (Department of Health 2004). While the current focus in the NHS is on more physical problems, mental health will have to be addressed in the not too distant future. But here it appears that we have come full circle. Much of the professionalization of counselling is attributable to therapists in independent practice offering their services to GPs who paid them through a variety of creative funding streams, for example through the auxiliary workers' budgets. Many of these therapists subsequently left private work to become part of managed teams in primary care.

Now with the advent of PBC they could once more find themselves offering their services to GPs for a fee. The difference is that now there are stringent guidelines to which GP practices must adhere in order to justify using their budget for PBC. These include clinical governance (particularly evidence-based practice which currently is dominated by Cognitive Behavioural Therapy CBT), audit and evidence of a clear management structure. This move has clear implications for independent practitioners who may well have to hone their more integrative skills and become more familiar with audit and initiatives such as those proposed by Layard (2006). It is easy to imagine that it will be the larger providers who will offer this, with individual therapists being subsumed into the service. In the USA with the HMO model, a plethora of small providers started offering a variety of services. However, within a few years these providers were merged into a small number of large providers who now dominate US mental health provision. Will this be the shape of things to come in the UK?

Development of training enterprises

The movement of therapists into the health-care arena had a reflective effect on the pressure for regulation. Working in a formal context, as in the USA, brought a greater demand for accreditation of therapists to a minimum qualification standard, along with associated requirements of minimum levels of supervision, insurance and continuing professional development (CPD). Whether a therapist should also have minimum levels of personal therapy was then, and still is today, a hotly debated issue. Entrepreneurial institutions and universities saw a niche in the training market to meet the demand of those wanting to be counsellors and psychotherapists. Many people were drawn to the prospect of being able to set up in private practice and dictate the terms and conditions of one's own employment. However, it takes a good three years to establish a private practice of meaningful size. At the same time practitioners also moved into primary care, as therapists became more established in the NHS, which provided a regular income and established a GP referral base. In order to be accepted into primary care they had to have qualifications, so the demand for training increased and a self-fulfilling cycle was set up. The result was that the market was flooded with training courses and people trained in some form of counselling or psychotherapy, leaving psychoanalysis as a minority model within the talking cures.

The effect of the rapid expansion of training courses had a two-tiered effect. First, there were geographical pockets around the UK where training courses were based, e.g. London or Bristol, where there were too many trained therapists chasing too few counselling posts. As a result, the therapists would fall back into the position of being forced into private practice by default. As many of the employed therapists also undertook private work in addition to their primary care work, this left the sole private practitioners competing for clients and earning insufficient income to make a living. In such circumstances self-employment can have its downside and can place pressure on the therapist who has to pay a mortgage. In this case the therapist may encourage clients to stay in therapy longer than they need to (Hudson-Allez 1999), or may skimp on continuing professional development requirements (CPD) or supervision. In Chapter 10, Rosalind Field explores further the dangers of fiscal dependence of private practitioners upon their clients.

The managed care emphasis on brief models of therapy

The American HMOs also initiated the drive for brief and solution-focused therapies in managed care systems (Hoyt 1995), highlighting that the literature showed no real evidence base in outcome between short- or long-term therapy. It was argued that the real choice was not between long-term therapy or short-term therapy, but short-term therapy versus no therapy at all, as finances were not limitless. Cummings (1977) elaborated on this trend and reflected on the dichotomy between the idealism of long-term work in private practice and the short-term realism required in the HMO. But the American model had fierce critics who point out how HMOs have eroded confidentiality ethics and have sub-ordinated the therapists' clinical judgements in their pressure to save (and to make) money (Bollas and Sundelson 1995). Adrian Hemmings discusses further the threats to confidentiality in Chapter 5.

The NHS in the UK appeared to follow suit. Auditors were fearful that counselling in primary health care would open the floodgates for anxious and neurotic people to sit for years in therapy at the taxpayers' expense. So the vast majority of primary care trusts' (PCTs) managed counselling services impose a time limit on the therapist–patient contract – most typically six, 10 or 12 sessions (Hudson-Allez 1997). Some have been even more stringent, and I have knowledge of some services that limit the contact to two sessions and others that limit the therapeutic hour of 50 minutes down to 20 minutes.

As therapists have merged into medical settings they are surrounded by a problem-solving biomedical model that may be at odds with their own theoretical model (Totton 1997). The demands of counselling in primary care are high. The assessment stage requires knowledge and skills that can challenge the most experienced therapist, as the range of presenting issues can be vast. What is interesting here is how the therapist then starts to change and adapt his or her method of working to suit the demands of the context. The requirement for working within a time limit has led to therapists seeking more training in brief and time-limited approaches (House 1996). There is an increased use of the mind–body connection and a trend toward integrative models to get the therapy to fit the patient, rather than the other way round. Over time the therapists change their practice and they request CPD on the use of medication, on clinical assessment (using a diagnosis model), and legal and ethical dilemmas. Thus they search for training in pragmatic issues instead of theoretical depth.

Bor and McCann (1999) reinforce this process and highlight the trajectory of specialism of primary care counselling, as it resolves the paradoxes of working within a team yet maintaining confidentiality, sometimes needing to be directive with patients whilst honouring the traditions of psychotherapy. In addition, the therapist is trying to deal with such a diverse range of patient presenting issues, yet also to fit within the narrow demands of evidence-based practice. Thus it seems that counselling in a primary care setting has emerged as a distinct discipline in its own right (Hudson-Allez 2000). This is a movement away from being an independent practitioner to one of a group of professionals that forms part of the primary or secondary health-care teams. Being a team player can affect the whole ethos of the therapeutic frame. In addition, the so-called free primary health care for the patient leads to a high non-attendance rate for GP consultations, and equally so for the primary care therapist.

The professionalization of counselling and psychotherapy

As already discussed, the demand for regulation and minimum standards of qualifications for therapists and psychotherapists has led to the emergence of numerous training courses, churning out therapists trained in popular theoretical models. In turn, this has led to a standardization of theoretical approach as to how therapy is presumed to be conducted, and in a way counselling has lost a lot of the uniqueness that highlighted the therapy of 30 years ago. In addition the convergence of therapists into medical and corporate settings has led to the professionalization of talking cures by default. When therapists fought with ambivalent accountants and auditors in health authorities to maintain their position within primary care, strict guidelines were created to protect the profession internally from the critical attacks from outside. Thus came the establishment of professional bodies that are context specific, first CPC and later the Faculty of Healthcare Counsellors and Psychotherapists (FHPC), an offshoot of the BACP. These organizations developed protocols and guidelines of safe practice for the therapist working within the health service (CPC 1999), and to reassure the government of the professionalism of the work and to maintain clinical governance. However, in the need for professional bodies to demonstrate the professional identity of its members, it does invite competition between the bodies as they jostle for position between their membership and the Department of Health.

The emergence of a professional body means that it can advocate methods of self-regulation by setting standards of training and competency to practice. Yet following contemporary difficulties within the British Medical Association (BMA), some people are suspicious of the concept of self-regulation and are arguing for a more formal regulation of counselling and psychotherapy via the Health Professionals Council, the Council for Professions Allied with Medicine, or some other dedicated mental health council. This is currently under debate, but again stumbles across the difficulties of psychotherapy not being a unitary profession; although the Department of Health have intimated that they want regulation with a light touch and will maintain a distinction between counselling and psychotherapy as two separate professions (Foster 2006).

There have been some very positive aspects of this professionalism. It provides (some) protection for the patient, who sees a therapist in the surgery in good faith, on the understanding that the GP would not have referred him or her to the therapist if the person had not been suitably qualified and experienced to receive the referral. The therapist too feels supported by an organization like CPC, which is working to enhance their working conditions and establishing boundaries of good practice. This can lead to the increased likelihood of positive outcomes for work undertaken. The GP and the employing PCTs then feel reassured that they have protected themselves as best they can from the threat of a negligence tort. It also establishes good terms and conditions and links the professional therapist into the same schema of working conditions and status as other health professionals; hence the inclusion of counsellors in the negotiation of the Department of Health's Agenda for Change salary ratings.

On the negative side, managed care services have often moved into a form of defensive practice. For example, some PCTs have required their therapists to immediately re-refer any patient who expresses any form of suicidal ideation to the secondary service community mental health team (CMHT) for a psychiatric referral. This requirement stems not from clinical need, as the therapist is more than able to assess suicidal risk in his or her own right, but from a fear of litigation; that the patient might self-harm and then the PCT be held negligent and liable after a complaint from a distressed family. This leads into greater erosion of the confidentiality ethic between therapist and patient, and pathologizes what are sometimes reasonably normal expressions of despair. It also creates an idea that there is an ideal treatment or management solution somewhere else in the NHS, which is not always the case and can result in patients being passed around the system.

Evidence-based practice versus practice-based evidence

One of the downsides of professionalization is the fiscal demand for evidence-based therapy. Although it is a laudable argument that it is futile paying good money for certain forms of therapy if they have not been proven to be effective, the argument only has validity when there are adequate methods of researching the therapy. Hemmings (2000) cogently argues on the difficulties encountered when researchers blur the boundaries between the controlled environments of an efficacy study versus the real-life research into effectiveness. It is clearly impossible to use a controlled methodological model (randomly controlled trials, RCTs, being the gold standard) used for drug efficacy to what is essentially a narrative process. What the push for RCTs does lose sight of, however, is that much of the published literature providing the evidence base was initiated by the practice base before the profession was formalized. Thus the practice base had led to the raising of hypotheses, leading to evaluation and evidence-based outcomes. Nevertheless, it has not prevented the overinvolvement of auditors into methods of therapy by the repetitive demands for Cognitive Behavioural Therapy (CBT) over and above other techniques as this therapy, being more manualized with the use of proforma and protocols, is able to lend itself preferentially to efficacy research. As any clinician knows, CBT, whilst being an effective form of therapy with some presenting problems, is not the panacea for all ills. Yet even here there is some selective attention to the outcome literature. In an RCT of CBT, non-directive (presumably person-centred) counselling and usual GP care for the treatment of depression and anxiety, Ward *et al.* (2000) found that there was no difference between CBT or non-directive therapy, but both were clinically significantly more effective than usual GP care in the short but not the long term.

This love affair with CBT does not just manifest in PCTs trying to influence the way the therapist works, it has also impacted on the views of the government, hence the Department of Health introducing primary care mental health workers (PCMHWs) into some primary care areas. These are graduate psychologists or social science graduates with an academic degree and no clinical experience, who are sent on a short course of CBT and then moved into primary care, ostensibly to work alongside or in some areas even replace the therapist. The paradox here is that, as previously mentioned, PCTs are encouraging therapists to be defensive in their practice for fear of litigation, yet the government are placing themselves at such risk by encouraging the use of inexperienced clinicians at the coalface.

Impact of employee assistance programmes

Another entrepreneurial enterprise following from the United States is the employee assistance programme (EAP). These are companies that liaise between employers and therapists to offer support and help to the company's staff. By taking a large, regular financial payment from the company, an EAP can pay therapists a much smaller sum to see the referred clients. But again, as with any organizational approach to therapy or treatment, companies are mindful of mistakes and fearful of civil torts of negligence. Therefore they insist on a minimum level of qualification and supervision, and usually restrict the number of counselling sessions to which the client is entitled to six. There are also some that will only refer patients to the therapist if the therapist conducts a certain form of therapy, for example, Cognitive Behavioural Therapy.

In addition, EAPs may require the therapists to sign inappropriate contractual obligations, for example, taking away any copyright of any writing or literature the therapist may undertake, or even taking away their 'moral rights', sometimes demanding that the therapists give their clients priority attention, which overrides the therapists' clinical assessment of patient need. The contract also does not allow the therapist to continue working with the same client on a private basis, even if the client asks for this and is willing to pay. Others require their therapists to complete written reports on each session undertaken, which are then sent through the post to the company. One wonders if the clients are aware that their personal information is being sent to an unnamed person in an unnamed company to be accumulated in a file of which they are also unaware, and the implications of this under the Data Protection Act. Thus there is a concomitant erosion of confidentiality and sometimes the EAP may be based too close to the employer or within the employer's premises.

The result of this is that some private practitioners, who may be fearful of not gaining enough client referrals to keep a private practice viable, sign up to EAPs that then disempower them. The organizations do this by regulating the client–therapist contracts, dictating the level of administration undertaken and therefore eroding professional working ethics. The positive side of EAPs, however, is that they provide the struggling private practitioner with a referral base. The better EAP organizations offer support for the therapist in the form of additional clinical support, legal and financial advice and additional training. Some therapists take advantage of the organizations by charging a greater fee than they do their private clients (Friery 2003). Melanie Withers discusses more about this effect on the work of the therapist in Chapter 4 on assessment.

Impact on the voluntary sector

The original basis of counselling in the UK was formulated in the voluntary sector, but in recent times it has been increasingly squeezed out by the professionalization of therapists. As many volunteers do not have to have minimum levels of qualification, the tendency is that they use counselling skills as opposed to being a professional therapist. This is not meant to undermine the importance of being able to give a listening ear to someone when they are distressed. However, there is always the danger that the volunteer, being untrained in assessment processes, is likely to commence counselling when it may be inappropriate to do so, for example, if the person has a deep-seated issue or a personality disorder.

Professional therapists argue that volunteers, because by their very nature they have some other form of income, are therefore predominantly from a middle-class background, not having true insight into the real difficulties of the working class. Other professional therapists feel threatened by people who are prepared to do the same job as them for no money, as it puts their livelihood under threat. Similarly, there is a surfeit of therapists coming off the training course conveyor belt looking for clinical hours to clock up in order to gain sufficient experience for accreditation. Therefore there are always therapists who are willing to work for no recompense (see Rosalind Field and Adrian Hemming's further discussion on this in Chapter 9).

In some cases, it has been found that the therapist has actually paid the GP for the privilege of working in the surgery (Friery 2003). This has not gone unnoticed by fiscal auditors who would rather get therapists to do the job for nothing or use trainee placements than pay a therapist a professional wage. Primary care or university counselling are common targets for the student therapist. Such placements have an abundance of potential clients and the accreditation hours can add up quite rapidly. However, this has been open to abuse as PCTs have expected the trainees to provide their own external supervision without providing any in-house mentoring or support. Here again is the paradox between the aforementioned defensive practice for fear of litigation, yet the PCTs are putting themselves open to risk of malpractice by using unskilled labour in order to save money.

Impact of the law on the therapist

One unexpected influence on the way therapists and psychotherapists work has come from the legal profession. This is one occasion where we differ from the United States. There the law protects confidentiality between therapist and client, whereas in the UK the only confidentiality ethic protected by law is the lawyers' own legal privilege. For the UK therapist there are already statutory obligations to breach confidentiality, with the threat of personal prosecution under the Terrorism Act, Drug Trafficking Act and the new Criminal Justice Bill if we fail to comply. Furthermore, the legal profession and the police have realized that therapists have access to a considerable amount of useful information, and are constantly making requests for copies of the therapist's notes for civil and criminal litigation. Although therapists are at liberty to say no to them, lawyers only need to go to a judge for an order and the therapist then has no choice but to comply or risk a prosecution for contempt of court (Young and Hudson-Allez 2005).

The threat that a therapist never knows when they will receive a demand for a copy of their notes, either from the client under the Data Protection Act (Jenkins 2002) or from the legal profession, has impacted upon how a therapist actually behaves as part of the therapy (Hudson-Allez 2004b). Therapists are now acting defensively in terms of note-taking, changing a reflective practice in the writing of copious notes as part of the therapeutic understanding of the process into brief factual notes where reflection and countertransference issues, etc. are inhibited and confined to verbal exchanges between supervisor and supervisee. Thus, thinking about the client in readiness for the next session changes.

Impact of change on private practice

How have all these changes impacted on the practitioner who chooses to stay in private practice? There are many therapists who are still vehemently opposed to regulation, viewing the whole procedure as anti-therapeutic (Totton 1997). In private practice, as yet anyway, there is no requirement for minimum training requirements. As Friery (2003) points out, there are still a significant number of therapists practising who are not trained in any recognizable way. Most private practitioners do belong to a professional body, and as such are required to abide by their respective code of ethics (Bond 2000). However, there is no obligation for any practitioner working independently to do so. They have the luxury of being able to be theoretically purist without the pressure of having restrictions on session numbers, providing their practice is sufficiently large not to have to apply for referrals. However, they may be putting themselves at personal risk by separating themselves from the majority who follow the regulatory route. Should a current or former client make a negligence claim against them, the lawyers in a civil tort would apply the Bolam Test in court. This is an analysis of the behaviour of the practitioner in relation to other skilled practitioners in the same field. If the majority of therapists and psychotherapists follow the minimum standards as laid down by regulatory authorities, a practitioner can be considered negligent if he or she practises without those minimum requirements (Jenkins 1997; Hudson-Allez 2004a).

In the United States, the movement of therapists into HMOs has led to a decline in the number of private practitioners. This is not the case in the UK so far. However, the increasing use of therapists in primary care has had a domino effect on to private practice. As mentioned, many therapists work in both health care and private settings. But for therapists who choose to work privately alone, they then have to deal with the expectations of their client. It may be that a client's first experience of counselling was the six sessions he or she experienced at the surgery, and is now looking to deal with more issues in greater depth. This sets up expectations of ways of working that may be completely different to the private practitioner. Such clients may also expect letters and reports written for free, as is so often the case within primary care. The increase in NHS counselling has also impacted on the provision of private supervision, and in particular the nature of supervision with supervisors increasingly having to be aware of NHS structures, constraints, legal obligations and ethical matters arising from work in this setting (Murphy *et al.* 2002).

Of course there are other essential differences between working in a health-care context and working in private practice. In the latter there is more time for self-analysis and reading in a quiet atmosphere, as opposed to the hustle and bustle of a general practice with just ten minutes between patients. It may also be more possible to make an authentic therapeutic alliance in a private setting without the third party element of the GP practice impinging on the alliance. Some patients may feel freer to use therapy in the private frame. The attendance rate is different too. Clients rarely do not turn up in private practice when they have to pay for the therapy, as there is more personal investment in it, whereas in primary care the non-attendance rate may be anywhere between 10 and 25 per cent.

The CPD options chosen by practitioners in the private sector as compared to NHS-funded therapists may also be different. For private practitioners, these options are more likely to be theoretical rather than pragmatic. The private practitioner has to pay for his her own supervision, insurance and CPD, again discussed by Rosalind Field and Adrian Hemmings in Chapter 9. However, on the positive side, the independent practitioner can choose a supervisor who is independent and objective, whereas a PCT or EAP may insist on supervision being conducted with a (suitably qualified) person of their choice. There may even be a blurring of boundaries with the supervisor having dual roles of clinical supervisor and line manager.

Conclusion

There has been a rapid rate of change in counselling, certainly more so in the last decade than in the previous two. Developments of US managed care systems and brief therapy models have been mirrored in the UK, but as is often the case, the UK may choose to take the cheapest routes. The increasing use of therapists in primary care has led to a merging of theoretical orientation to cope with the demands of the context and session restrictions, thus leaving the therapists who choose to stay in private practice adhering to the more purist models of therapy in accordance with their training modality. For the most part, primary care counselling has emerged into a new form of integrative therapy, with the therapist using a toolkit of interventions for various presenting problems that allow and enhance short-term therapy to deal with emotional distress. As the NHS rarely provides unlimited therapy to patients, it leaves the deeper and longer term personal analysis for the private sector.

References

Balint, M. (1974) *The Doctor, his Patient, and the Illness*, Edinburgh: Pitman Medical.

Baron, J. (1996) The emergence of counselling as a profession, in R. Bayne, I. Horton and J. Bimrose (eds) *New Directions in Counselling*, London: Routledge, pp. 16–24.

Bollas, C. and Sundelson, D. (1995) *The New Informants: The Betrayal of Confidentiality in Psychoanalysis and Psychotherapy*, Northville, NJ: Jason Aronson.

Bond, T. (2000) *Standards and Ethics for Counselling in Action*, London: Sage.

Bor, R. and McCann, D. (1999) Introduction, in R. Bor and D. McCann (eds) *The Practice of Counselling in Primary Care*, London: Sage.

Counsellors and Psychotherapists in Primary Care (CPC, 1999) *Professional Counselling and Psychotherapy. Guidelines and Protocols*, Bognor Regis: CPC.

Cummings, N. (1977) Prolonged (ideal) versus short-term (realistic) psychotherapy, *Professional Psychology* 4: 491–501.

Department of Health (2004) *Practice based commissioning: Promoting Clinical Engagement*, London: Department of Health.

Frankland, A. (1997) Professional recognition: accreditation and reaccredidation, in P. Wilkins (ed.) *Personal and Professional Development for Counsellors*, London: Sage, pp. 50–64.

Foster, J. (2006) Chair of Counsellors and Psychotherapists in Primary Care, personal communication.

Friery, K. (2003) The price of counselling, *Counselling and Psychotherapy Journal* 14(8): 7–9.

Hemmings, A. (2000) A systematic review of research into psychological interventions in primary health care, *Family Systems and Health* 18: 279–313.

House, R. (1996) The professionalisation of counselling: a coherent case against?, *Counselling Psychology Quarterly* 9(4): 343–358.

Hoyt, M. F. (1995) *Brief Therapy and Managed Care. Readings for Contemporary Practice*, San Francisco: Jossey-Bass.

Hudson, G. (1988) Counsellors within general practice: time and need for utilization, credibility and accreditation, *Counselling Psychology Review* 3(1): 15–20.

Hudson-Allez, G. (1997) *Time-Limited Therapy in a General Practice Setting*, London: Sage.

—— (1999) Brief versus open-ended counselling in primary care. Should the service be expanded to include both models?, *European Journal of Psychotherapy, Counselling and Health* 2(1): 7–18.

—— (2000) What makes counsellors working in primary care distinct from counsellors working in other settings?, *British Journal of Guidance and Counselling* 28(2): 203–213.

—— (2004a) *Safe Practice: Legal Issues for Psychological Therapists*, Bognor Regis: Counsellors and Psychotherapists in Primary Care.

—— (2004b) Threats to psychotherapeutic confidentiality: can psychotherapists in the UK really offer a confidentiality ethic to their clients?, *Psychodynamic Practice* 10(3): 317–331.

Jenkins, P. (1997) *Counselling, Psychotherapy and the Law*, London: Sage.

—— (2002) Transparent recording: therapists and the Data Protection Act, in P. Jenkins (ed.) *Legal Issues in Counselling and Psychotherapy*, London: Sage, pp. 45–56.

Layard, R. (2006) The case for psychological treatment centres, *British Medical Journal* 332: 1030–1032.

Mowbray, R. (1995) *The Case Against Psychotherapy Registration: A Conservation Issue for the Human Potential Movement*, London: Trans Marginal.

Murphy, A., Butterworth, M. and Foster, J. (2002) *Supervision of*

Psychological Therapists Working in Primary Care, 2nd edn, Bognor Regis: Counsellors and Psychotherapists in Primary Care.

Totton, N. (1997) Inputs and outcomes: the medical model and professionalism, *Self and Society* 25(4): 38.

Ward, E., King, M., Lloyd, M., Bower, P., Sibbald, B., Farrelly, S. *et al.* (2000) Randomised controlled trial of non-directive counselling, cognitive-behaviour therapy and usual general practitioner care in the management of depression as well as mixed anxiety and depression in primary care, *British Medical Journal* 321: 1383–1388.

Wilkin, D., Gillam, S. and Leese, B. (eds) (1999) *The National Tracker Survey of Primary Care Groups and Trusts. Progress and Challenges 1999/2000*, Manchester: University of Manchester.

Young, T. and Hudson-Allez, G. (2005) *Writing Reports and Giving Evidence in Court*, Bognor Regis: Counsellors and Psychotherapists in Primary Care.

Chapter 3

Advertising

Lawrence Suss

Introduction

Setting up in private practice carries the risk of falling at the first hurdle – no clients – and it is therefore bound to make anyone anxious. If you are taking the step of setting up a private practice you will probably be faced with the thorny questions of 'Just where will I get my clients?' or 'How will people get to know what I offer?', or some such question that might keep you awake at night. Succeeding in private practice depends upon building a steady stream of reliable clients. This chapter begins to try to identify how you might maximize your chances of getting referrals.

Of course, it goes without saying that the best advertisement is good, ethical practice where clients feel that their concerns have been heard and go away feeling different from when they came. These clients will remember the support and help you have offered and will be likely to pass your name to others who are seeking counselling. It is also worth bearing in mind the opposite effect: all it takes is a few very disgruntled clients to spread rumours of your incompetence or unethical practice and potential clients will stay away. I am going to assume that you will practise wisely, ethically and effectively with appropriate clients. (I am not going to enter the debate about what is 'effective' counselling in this chapter: this is a matter discussed at length elsewhere.)

The content of this chapter is written with some trepidation as at least in part it has the potential rapidly to become out of date. Perhaps the chapter should carry a health warning to readers, namely to remember to check that what is written is still the case. This is especially true for extracts from the codes of ethics of various professional bodies that have been quoted and for internet addresses (URLs) on that ever-changing beast the internet. This chapter aims to bring together three important aspects of what could crudely be called advertising:

- the codes of ethics under which counsellors and psychotherapists may make known to the public what they have to offer
- the places where counsellors and therapists might consider placing details of what they offer in order that members of the public might seek their services
- the more philosophical question of what is appropriate to say about oneself when setting out one's wares in this way.

The reader might already have picked up my struggle with the use of the word 'advertising' as opposed to 'making the public aware of what is on offer'. This is because to be seen directly to advertise is a contentious issue (and unethical) for some professional bodies. Of course what is or is not an advertisement is open to debate and will be considered in the third part of this chapter.

Finally, the ideas for action below can seem daunting to anyone who has not had to market themselves before. I have been involved in counsellor training since 1989 and in my experience those trainees who have been strategic and invested time and energy in building a practice have usually succeeded. Those who have been reticent and held back have often failed. It might be important for you to seek some professional support during the time you are trying to build your private practice. You might want to use your personal counsellor or therapist, your supervisor or even approach a life coach.

The ethical position

In this section what I mean by the ethical position is simply this: what do the codes of ethics of the British Association for Counselling and Psychotherapy (BACP) and the United Kingdom Council for Psychotherapy (UKCP) have to say about advertising? What can you do to make the public aware of what you offer without fear of being censured by your professional body or at worst being struck off? On 1st April 2002, the BACP adopted the Ethical Framework for Good Practice in Counselling and Psychotherapy, which unlike earlier BACP codes does not spell out the conditions under which members may advertise their services. The focus of the new code is based upon underlying ethical values and principles and members are left to draw out for themselves how advertisements may be framed. The closest the framework comes to dealing with advertising is in the section entitled 'Probity in Professional Practice' which states:

52. All information about services should be honest, accurate, avoid unjustifiable claims, and be consistent with maintaining the good standing of the profession.
53. Particular care should be taken over the integrity of presenting qualifications, accreditation and professional standing.

(BACP, 2002: 9)

These two paragraphs deal with both the contracting aspects of your work with clients and with the pre-counselling information, that is, your advertising. In short, however you decide to advertise you must not misrepresent or over-egg your qualifications or professional standing. You must not make any claims to cure people (no matter how appealing it might be for you to think that you can, for example, stop all people smoking or help everyone with their bereavement issues). You must not make unnecessary and unfavourable comparisons between your style and approach to counselling and that of another school or approach. You must certainly not say that you are better than anyone else.

At first reading, paragraph 53 appears to repeat the same theme as paragraph 52. However, it does so with greater specificity about which areas you must take special care over when you provide details for the public. I think that paragraph 53 carries further meaning than just dealing with the content of what is said in an advertisement. It also deals (tangentially) with the process. By this I mean that our advertisements need to be not only ethical in terms of content but also in terms of style of presentation. When you are designing the layout, type fonts and use of graphics need to be appropriate in style to an advertisement about counselling.

The published BACP policy on advertising (to be found on the BACP website and reproduced in edited form in Figure 3.1) focuses on how organizations, individuals and trainers can use the name of BACP and BACP accreditation to describe themselves or the courses they offer. The site offers no guidance on any other matter.

Member's Advertising Policy

All members are bound by BACP's Ethical Framework for Good Practice in Counselling and Psychotherapy, the Ethical Guidelines for Researching Counselling and Psychotherapy (where practitioners undertake research) and subject to the Professional Conduct Procedure for the time being in force. This should be reflected in all promotional literature.

The use of designatory letters and advertising statements

Designatory letters are to be used to clarify the level of membership and should not be used to infer that membership of BACP is a qualification.

Accredited Membership MBACP (Snr. Accred)

Accredited Members who have applied and met the criteria for Senior Accredited Counsellor/Psychotherapist, Supervisor or Trainer may use the designatory letters MBACP (Snr. Accred) and should describe themselves as

- BACP Senior Accredited Counsellor/Psychotherapist*
- BACP Senior Accredited Supervisor*
- BACP Senior Accredited Trainer*

* whichever is applicable.

Accredited Membership MBACP (Accred)

Members in this category may use the designatory letters MBACP (Accred). Counsellors, Supervisors, and Trainers accredited by BACP should make it clear in any literature produced the specific area they are accredited in by describing themselves as either:

- BACP Accredited Counsellor/Psychotherapist*
- BACP Accredited Supervisor*
- BACP Accredited Trainer

* whichever is applicable.

Member BACP (MBACP)

Members in this category may use the designatory letters MBACP providing they have submitted evidence that they have successfully completed a minimum of one year full time or two year part time counselling and/or psychotherapy course which includes a supervised placement.

Member (no designatory letters)

This category is for members who have not completed or have not submitted the required qualifications for the member MBACP category. Members in this category may **not** use any designatory letters.

Members in this category may describe themselves:

"As a Member of BACP I am bound by its Ethical Framework for Good Practice in Counselling and Psychotherapy, the Ethical Guidelines for Researching Counselling and Psychotherapy (where practitioners undertake research) and subject to the Professional Conduct Procedure for the time being in force."

Associate Membership (no designatory letters)

Members in this category may **not** use designatory letters.

Members in this category may describe themselves:

"As an Associate Member of BACP I am bound by its Ethical Framework for Good Practice in Counselling and Psychotherapy, the Ethical Guidelines for Researching Counselling and Psychotherapy (where practitioners undertake research) and subject to the Professional Conduct Procedure for the time being in force."

Student membership (no designatory letters)

Members in this category may **not** use designatory letters

Members in this category may describe themselves:

"As a Student Member of BACP I am bound by its Ethical Framework for Good Practice in Counselling and Psychotherapy, the Ethical Guidelines for Researching Counselling and Psychotherapy (where practitioners undertake research) and subject to the Professional Conduct Procedure for the time being in force."

Affiliate Membership (no designatory letters)

Members in this category may **not** use designatory letters.

Members in this category may describe themselves:

"As an Affiliate Member of BACP I am bound by its Ethical Framework for Good Practice in Counselling and Psychotherapy, the Ethical Guidelines for Researching Counselling and Psychotherapy (where practitioners undertake research) and subject to the Professional Conduct Procedure for the time being in force."

Organisational members (no designatory letters)

Organisational members may **not** use designatory letters

Members in this category may describe themselves:

"As an Organisational of BACP we are bound by its Ethical Framework for Good Practice in Counselling and Psychotherapy, the Ethical Guidelines for Researching Counselling and Psychotherapy (where practitioners undertake research) and subject to the Professional Conduct Procedure for the time being in force."

However not simply as: "An Organisational Member of BACP."

The Misuse of Designatory Letters

Members found to be using the designatory letters when not permitted to do so, or using them in a manner that is inconsistent with the right of use, and/or suggesting explicitly or by implication that the use of such letters represents a qualification of any kind, may be subject to the Association's Professional Conduct Procedures and/or have their continuing membership of the Association considered by the Board of Governors under powers derived from the Memorandum & Articles of Association. This may include the imposition of sanctions up to and including the termination of membership of BACP. BACP is the proprietor of the UK Trade Mark for the letters and any misuse thereof would constitute trade mark infringement.

April 2005

Figure 3.1 BACP policy on advertising

Source: Reproduced by kind permission of BACP (BACP website, March 2006)

UKCP have taken a different approach. Following internal pressure from members, in 2000 the UKCP published a policy statement about websites (see Figure 3.2) and makes it very clear that psychotherapists are required to consider both content and form of advertising. Although this statement applies only to websites, it does provide a good guide to ethical practice in all other forms of advertising.

Part of acting ethically is being clear about the extent of your training and practising within your competence, and also being trained in any specialism you offer. If you intend to claim to work with clients with particular presentations, then you must ask yourself the question: 'If I had a professional complaint against me, would a fair-minded panel believe that I am adequately qualified to work with this particular client?' Although this sounds rather defensive and conservative, I suggest it is a good guide to follow when thinking about how you might describe your practice (and, of course, actually practise). Thinking about this might also help you to begin to be clearer about exactly what you offer and so take you one step nearer the material you might publish in a leaflet or on the web.

The sorts of information you might include in your advertising

What should be clear from the above is that you should be aiming to include basic factual information about yourself and what you offer. You might also want to include a statement of your philosophy or approach to your work, but to remain ethical this must make no claims for cure and must not say your approach is better than any other approach.

Thistle (1998) provides a good guide of what you might include in a leaflet that can also be seen to form the contract for the work. It is a descriptive style that could also be adapted for use on a webpage. If you wanted to go more to a list style and leave the contracting elements to a separate document, then the headings you should consider are as follows:

1   Name, the address where you practise, contact phone number (consider carefully if you also want to use your home and/or mobile numbers).

The Internet and Advertising

There have been a number of enquiries from those who are establishing web sites and from those who object to the web sites of colleagues. The growing use of the web as a form of communication and promotion/advertising causes us to need to address this issue. While at the same time the nature of communication on the net means that the second paragraph of our ethical requirements is challenged.

The UKCP Ethical Requirements for Member Organisations' states:

"Advertising: Member organisations of UKCP are required to restrict promotion of their work to a description of the type of psychotherapy they provide. Psychotherapists are required to distinguish carefully between self-descriptions, as in a list, and advertising seeking enquiries"

Web pages need to be seen not as advertising but as giving information. Our first reaction was that the web is ethically the same as any other medium, but that there were special considerations. We first thought about what we saw as acceptable to use on a web site and these were:

1. Descriptions of style, modality or specialism of the psychotherapy
2. Descriptions of location of the practice
3. Qualifications of practitioner/s
4. Any relevant or current training or CPD of practitioners
5. Mention of relevant Codes of Practice would be desirable

And as not acceptable:

1. Claims to cure
2. Claims to be better than others.

The special considerations specific to web sites are that it is acceptable to use the following as long as the Ethical Requirements are kept in mind:

A. Use of different font sizes
B. Use of different colours and blocks
C. Using motion in graphics
D. Links to colleagues and member organisations – with their consent
E. E-mail address outward, i.e. provides the e-mail address of others, as a link
F. E-mail address/phone number inward, i.e. providing author's own address and phone number for further contact.

There have also been a number of enquiries regarding UKCP's position / policy when it comes to our member organisations and registrants being allowed to advertise themselves as such on their own websites and in their own marketing material.

Therefore we have commissioned our creative agency to produce the following three marks which MO's and registrants can apply to use to establish themselves publicly as UKCP Registered.

Figure 3.2 UKCP policy on the internet and advertising

Source: Reproduced by kind permission of UKCP (UKCP website, March 2006)

2 Qualifications (you may choose to include dates and awarding bodies).
3 Professional memberships and accreditation.
4 Services offered (what sort of client groups you work with – individuals, couples, groups, organizations, etc.).
5 What sorts of issues you deal with in your work (e.g. depression, relationships).
6 Highlight any special interest or area in which you are qualified to work.
7 The code(s) of ethics under which you work (e.g. BACP, BAPPS). BACP have a suggested form of words for this (see Figure 3.1).

It is worth looking at the literature and websites of other counsellors and therapists to see what they include and how they present it. Webpages lend themselves to brief and factual statements, whereas leaflets (which clients can take away) can be more discursive. Also check how other practitioners describe counselling or psychotherapy. There is no one way to describe what we do and it is often hard to know where to start, so do some research on the web.

Making one's services known

It is important to be able to monitor the effectiveness of any marketing you undertake, as this will enable you to review on a regular basis (perhaps annually) how you should spend your time and money. I believe the best way to monitor your strategy is to ask all new clients where they got your name, and don't be too put off by vagueness, ask again if you are not clear. Remember, being in private practice is setting up your own business and no successful company would miss out on important marketing information. This means, for example, that if a potential client tells you that they contacted you because they got your name from a leaflet they picked up in their GP surgery, ask what was it about the leaflet that made them decide to contact you. Not only are you likely to get useful marketing information but the answer is also likely to be very helpful in your work together.

If a client tells you that a person referred them to you then take the time to thank the referrer. We all like to be acknowledged and a brief thanks on their answerphone is enough. There is a wide range of methods for a counsellor or psychotherapist to use to help promote a private practice. These include:

- inclusion in printed professional directories
- a personal website or joining an existing 'helping' site on the internet
- an entry in Yellow Pages or Thompson directory
- use of noticeboards or leaflet distribution in surgeries, health shops, alternative clinics and other health professionals
- use of focused direct mailing
- GP surgeries
- networking with colleagues, friends and family
- joining a local referral network
- advertising in newspapers and journals
- advertising on radio and television
- working in a voluntary organization
- supervision
- indirect marketing.

In the following sections I look at each heading separately but there is quite a lot of overlap between sections.

Inclusion in professional directories

The UKCP and BACP publish an annual listing of people offering counselling and/or psychotherapy. In the case of UKCP this is the list of qualified and registered UKCP psychotherapists and the cost is included in the annual registration fee. At its AGM in 2003, the UKCP agreed to establish a section to cover psychotherapeutic counselling, although the full details and implications in terms of which counsellors may join UKCP and who may be included in the register have (at the time of writing) yet to be resolved.

The BACP Directory is more flexible in that you do not have to be BACP accredited or UKCP registered to apply for inclusion. All members of BACP and previous entrants in the directory are circulated with details: the annual cost is £58 for members, £108 for non-members (from April 2005) for quite a detailed entry. The directory does distinguish between the entries of non-accredited and accredited counsellors.

The aim of UKCP and BACP is that their listings should find homes in local libraries and with voluntary counselling organizations so that members of the public looking for a counsellor or therapist can consult the list. In practice it is much less clear about how many libraries hold these up-to-date lists, although for the 2004 edition the BACP did target libraries. It is possible for members of the public to contact both UKCP and BACP via the web for electronically held details of the registers. BACP provides an interactive list of their directory allowing real-time searches (in 2005 the BACP website had around 83,000 hits per month and its Find a Therapist pages got just under 30,000 hits per month). UKCP invites you to email details of what you are looking for and they respond with the information. At the time of writing, the UKCP was developing its own interactive pages with details of how to find a therapist. In the meantime, a number of member organizations within UKCP list their members on their own webpages.

There are many regional counselling organizations in the UK, some of which publish directories of members with the express aim of seeking referrals for their members. These directories might be circulated locally including to GP surgeries, voluntary organizations, CAB and local libraries. Sometimes these published directories are also backed up by a real-time, web-based directory. The next section focuses on this.

I have used all three of the above: I am on the UKCP register, in the BACP Directory and in the local Sussex Counselling Directory. The total number of contacts from these sources has not been very great for me, perhaps two or three per year, but this could say more about the nature of what I have said about myself in these entries rather than the efficacy of this means of getting my name in front of the public.

A personal website or joining an existing 'helping' site on the internet

The internet has forced itself into almost everyone's life and has had a dramatic effect on the way that business and trade are done. Counsellors and psychotherapists are not immune and might want to turn this to their advantage. Thousands of people looking for goods and services use their favourite search engine as the starting point for finding what they want, and finding a counsellor comes into this category.

Most internet service providers (ISPs) allow their subscribers to have a homepage and it is usually possible to use this homepage as a website on which to make your services known. Writing webpages to create your own site can be fun, if you are that way inclined, or you can ask a professional to help you create one. You will have to prepare all the text and have some idea of the layout and colours you want in order to brief the person writing the code for the webpages. It is important to spend some time searching the net for examples of the pages other counsellors and therapists have published. If you particularly like someone's site, then make a note of the address (what is called the URL) so that your web designer can also have a look. Good pages are created by discussion, negotiation and looking at what other people have done.

Some counsellors have taken this a step further and purchased a domain name to use as the address (URL) for their site. Examples of domain names are www.bacp.co.uk for BACP or www.psychotherapy.org.uk for UKCP. A good domain name is easy to remember and allows potential clients to understand the link between the name of the site and what is on offer. However, domain names cost money and you will need to check with your ISP that they host your domain (i.e. they will allow you to park your website on their server). Choosing a domain name has been made easier by the many companies that sell them. Using your favourite search engine set to search the UK only, search for 'domain names for sale' and you should have returned a long list of possible name sellers. By opening some of these sites you will eventually find a system that allows you to check if the domain name you fancy has already been registered to another person.

For individuals in private practice the sort of domain you should be looking for is probably of the *.org.uk* sort where your domain name goes at the front (rather like the UKCP URL). The domain sort *.co.uk* tends to be used only for limited companies (which BACP is). Annual registration of a domain name is around £7.50 and if your existing ISP will not host your new domain then the company selling you the name almost certainly will. Some companies will charge for hosting your website but you should be able to find a good deal by searching.

One of the advantages of having purchased a domain is that you can then have your email address associated with the domain name. For example, I have purchased the domain www.suss.org.uk which allows me to have the email address lawrence@suss.org.uk. In theory, even if I change my internet service provider all I have to do is transfer my domain name and my email address remains unchanged.

There is another way of gaining a presence on the web and that is through one or more of the many counselling forums that offer lists. Some of these forums are free but others are commercial and will want you to pay a fee for listing. You should check whether you are expected to pay and how much, but also subject the site to a careful scrutiny to see what sort of people are already listed. Bear in mind that some clients will choose a counsellor by the company they appear to keep. If you are listed, for example, alongside astrologers and tarot card readers you might discourage (or encourage) certain potential clients.

To find these forums you should use your favourite search engine. I have a few which I list below, but do recall my caveat at the start of this chapter – some of these might already have gone out of business (an example of which can be found at www. counsellinguk.co.uk).

- www.counselling.ltd.uk

  A registered charity operating a national register of UK counsellors. Participants are asked if they are willing to take the occasional low or no-fee client.

- www.uktherapists.com

  This forum offers a listing and appears to require £19.99 for one year and £29.99 for two years. I recall adding my name a number of years ago for free. My name is still there and I have never paid anything (famous last words!).

- www.touchanytown.com

  Here you can replace the 'anytown' part of URL with Brighton, Bristol, Cardiff, etc. It appears to be a free listing to which you can simply add your name online.

Many regional or local counselling organizations offer lists of their members. This would require you to join the organization and pay the appropriate fee. A few examples include:

- www.haoc.co.uk   the site of Hampshire
                                               Association for Counselling
- www.sussex-counselling.co.uk   the site of Sussex Counselling
- www.psychodynamic.net   the site of Sussex
                                               Psychodynamic Therapies

A search of the net for your local organization might bring rewards. If you are a member of an organization that does not have a website with a list of members, then you might suggest they join the internet age.

BACP have recently launched a web-hosting service for members. For £6 plus VAT per month you can have a webpage entry with your own domain name either as www.*yourname*.bacp.co.uk or www.*yourname*.counselling.co.uk. BACP also offers more sophisticated packages including hosting your existing domain or website, although the charges are not the cheapest available.

Yellow Pages and Thompson directories

BACP (strictly the UK Register of Counsellors, UKRC) and UKCP have arrangements with both these organizations that allow members to advertise in their local Yellow Pages or Thompson directories under a collective UKRC or UKCP advertisement. The strength of this sort of advertising is that they appear to have the backing of the relevant professional organization and members of the public looking for a counsellor or therapist might give more weight to the names they see in this block advertisement. To be included in the UKCP advertisement you are required to be UKCP registered and to be in the UKRC advertisement you are required to be an accredited member of BACP. UKCP and BACP pass the names of registrants/members to the Yellow Pages or Thompson directories who contact you direct.

The downside of entries in both these directories is the cost; for example to participate in the Yellow Pages block advertisement can cost around £200 per year. I have heard quite different reports on how effective advertising in these directories can be, so if you are able to participate in these block advertisements and decide to go ahead, I strongly advise you to monitor their effectiveness.

Participation in these two directories comes from the two organizations direct, from lists provided by UKCP and UKRC. If you want to be included then you should contact the organization to which you belong as it will have initiated the list of contacts.

It is possible to advertise in these directories as an individual and if you take a quick look at either of them you will see quite a list of names under 'counselling' or 'psychotherapy'. Before booking space in either directory, I strongly urge you to telephone some of the counsellors or therapists listed and introduce yourself. Ask them how many referrals they have received from clients who have found their name in the directory. Most will respond helpfully and a decision to advertise or not will probably become clear.

Use of focused direct mailing

Sending unsolicited letters to busy people usually results in the letter ending up in the wastepaper bin. Direct mailings to doctors, dentists, health visitors, solicitors, midwives, personnel managers of big companies and other groups in contact with potential client groups only works if there is a clear mutuality of interest. People who work in the sorts of professions I have listed, and those that you might identify yourself, are frequently very hard working and very pressed for time. In addition they are often bombarded with literature from other people seeking their attention for services they want to sell (including other counsellors).

Before you design your mailing and write the copy, you need to ask yourself the question: 'What will make my letter stand out from the others and get a positive response with this target group?' For example, with doctors you will need to be aware of whether there is already a counsellor in their surgery and also what the waiting list is like. You will also need to know about other counselling or therapy offered by the local NHS trust to whom the GP will refer, and what the waiting list is there. You might need to identify whether you can offer particular specialist help to this GP's patients. Armed with this information, you can then begin to prepare your mailing which highlights how you can help this GP. For example, you might be able to offer very short referral times so that the patient who is demanding regular consultation with the GP might be moved to see you instead, thus releasing the GP to see other patients. Many GPs and other professionals are not against counsellors in private practice earning their living this way but they will want to know why they should refer to you and how it can help them (see below for more about GPs).

A second example, solicitors, who are dealing with divorces or bereaved clients seeking advice about probate, might be willing to refer clients to someone with couples or mediation experience or someone experienced with Cruse or a similar organization. Again, you will have to do your homework to try to find out what support the solicitor already has in place – try asking their secretary who might oblige. You need to establish how your work might assist the solicitor so that some mutuality of interest can be identified and acknowledged. Dealing with other professionals in private practice themselves is sometimes slightly easier than approaching those who work in the public sector, but do not let this put you off.

In many ways it is easier to get your message across in a visit to your target audience than via a mailing. I would suggest initially you telephone a key person in the target's workplace to see if you can get a five-minute interview rather than just send a mailing. This is no easy feat to achieve but it can be done. You will need to have worked out your pitch (i.e. what you intend to say) very carefully and it should be very focused on mutuality. You should also arm yourself with details of research outcomes into the efficacy of counselling (for example, Roth and Fonagy 1996). Take your literature to any such meeting so that you can leave it behind for them to read at their leisure. Be prepared to follow up the interview immediately in writing to summarize what was said and then about a week later telephone to see if they have any outstanding questions or issues with which you can help them.

Use of noticeboards or leaflet distribution in surgeries, health shops, alternative clinics and other health professionals

By doing some legwork in your local community you can identify places where it is possible to place some leaflets about what you offer. Direct mailing of leaflets and notices can very easily fail (see above for why) and it is the personal touch that can often bring success. Go and talk with the managers of health shops and alternative clinics, to GP and dental practice managers. Find out what they will display and how much (if anything) they charge. Check out what the other leaflets or notices look like in the clinic or shop. Look at the style, size and impact as well as the content. If this all sounds like too much effort, then you may have to resign yourself to finding only a few clients through other means.

GP surgeries

Thistle (1998) provides some good ideas on how to try to make contact with GPs. His emphasis is on personal contact because of the clear value of building a relationship and of being able to tailor the counselling provision to particular GP practices. The idea of mutuality of interest cannot be emphasized strongly enough.

In the sections above I suggest you should do your homework before tailoring your mailing to the specific target. You should also try to get to meet the GP you want to impress. Their time will be in great demand and you will have to use all your wits to persuade them or the practice manager to have five minutes in the busy regular practice meeting. Use your five minutes wisely and be prepared to answer questions. Key points include:

- your qualifications and experience
- any specialisms you can offer
- how you can complement existing counselling services
- the sorts of clients they should consider referring to you
- how you might be able to help with their difficult patients
- if you offer long-term work, why the GP should think about this option in contrast to the short-term work offered in the surgery (you might identify a number of issues that short-term work is not always good at treating or give some brief examples of clients who have got on well in longer term work but would not have done so in short-term work).

Many GPs are not averse to making private referrals but they need to know who you are and what you offer. Equally, you need to be aware that most GPs work within the medical model of illness, including prescribing antidepressants. You will need to examine your own attitude toward this if you hope for a successful relationship with a GP.

If you are successful in getting a referral from a GP (or from anyone else) then you might want to think about making it your practice to write to the GP after the first session to say that the patient has arrived and thanks. You will, of course, have to be absolutely clear with your client that it is your normal practice to write to the referring GP. You could also consider writing at the end of your work together. Thank-you letters to GPs must be few and far between, so your letters will stand out.

Information provided in a GP referral letter can vary, but as a minimum it will usually include the client's name, address and date of birth together with some brief details of the presenting problem. It might also include a brief history of the problem and previous attempts at treatment. It needs to be borne in mind that patients have access to their NHS medical records (except in the very rare cases where it is considered not to be in their best interests) so any letters you or the GP write may be read by the patient. This is not the place to discuss the wider issues of access to records and the BACP Information Sheet 'Access to Records of Counselling and Psychotherapy' (Jenkins 2004) is very comprehensive.

Networking with colleagues, friends and family

If you live in the area where you undertook your training, then make sure that you have informal agreements with co-trainees about cross-referral. What is meant by this is that you refer anyone to them whom you are not able to take on as a client because you already know them or they are a relative. In return they do the same for you. I have known groups of three and four ex-students who have built practices from these beginnings.

It is also worth mentioning to family and friends that you are now seeking to establish a private practice and therefore their help would be welcomed. You will need to be clear with them that you would not see people you know but you do have a good referral network. It is possible to network beyond friends and family. Identify social groups or clubs you belong to and see if it possible to network there.

Joining a local referral network

Joining a local counselling organization might also help, but be aware that as well as being collaborative members of such organizations are also your competitors, something not frequently acknowledged (see Clark 2002 for a discussion of these issues). Usually such organizations are on the look-out for speakers or workshop leaders – make sure you have something that you can offer. You might also want to think about taking on a role in such an organization so that your profile is raised. Local referral networks sometimes have directories of members, including those available on the net. If they don't, volunteer to look into it.

Another possibility is to create your own network. By this I mean establishing a co-operative which can take all the usual steps to advertise but work as a group with an internal referral system; thus with one telephone number for clients to contact. Such a group could emphasize its individual strengths and might serve to reassure potential referrers and clients that there will be a counsellor who can best serve their individual concerns. One requirement for such a group to succeed would be an open and comprehensive agreement about all aspects of the group's systems and working procedures.

Advertising in newspapers and journals

It is possible to find advertisements for counsellors in newspapers and journals, particularly local newspapers and local alternative magazines. Rather like checking out the value of the Yellow Pages, I would telephone the advertiser and see what the rate of referrals is like. Alternative magazines are more likely to be of value in finding clients, but again, rather like putting your name on a web listing, you should check carefully what sort of other advertisements you are going to be alongside. Generally this sort of advert can be quite expensive.

You might want to think about writing an article for your local paper or magazine which mentions what you do. Editors are usually quite difficult to convince about commissioning such articles and you might have to take a chance and submit something hoping for success. If you do succeed, then you might get a small fee for the article. If this happens then follow it up with a phone call to see if the editor will take more.

Advertising on radio and television

I have never seen or heard an advertisement on the television or radio for a counsellor. The best sort of advertisement is to get yourself on air to talk about your pet concern which is related to counselling in some way. This is no easy task but it is worth bearing in mind that on the whole counsellors and psychotherapists are a shy and retiring bunch of people who do not usually put themselves forward to deal with the press. There are occasional trainings run by BACP on dealing with the press and unless you have prior experience, it might be best to start out by taking such a course.

Working in a voluntary organization

Although this appears to be out of place in a chapter on private practice, do read on. One of the ways that newly qualified counsellors establish themselves in an area is by offering their services as a volunteer in a voluntary organization. If you do this, several key groups of people will get to know of your practice: the managers and supervisors in the organization; the clients whom you see; and some of the referring agencies if you are required to liaise with them during or at the end of the work with a client.

The managers and supervisors are often in private practice themselves and there may be times when they have more client referrals than they can handle. Over time these people will get to know and have confidence in your work and you can let it be known that you are establishing a private practice.

Dealing with your clients in such an organization from the perspective of increasing your private work needs to be handled ethically and carefully. You must never suggest to a client that they leave the organization and come to see you privately. Such a move would breach both the organization's and BACP's code of ethics and would leave you open to a complaint of professional misconduct – not a happy start to life in private practice. What to hope for is that when work with you at the organization has properly finished, the client will have been pleased with the experience and will suggest your name to friends or colleagues. Some such referrals might come to you via the organization, but some might look you up on the web or in the phone book.

There will be an organizational protocol dealing with referring agencies which may or may not include you as the counsellor. Never go outside the protocol, even if you disagree with it. If the protocol does allow direct contact between you and the referrer, then make sure your supervisor understands what is happening and agrees every step of the way. The sort of contact I have in mind is, for example, a letter to a GP saying that the work has now finished. Bearing in mind the need for confidentiality, such letters should be discussed and agreed with the client.

If you do write this sort of letter then the referring agency will know your name. It is possibly not unethical to write separately in a private capacity to the referring agency to let them know you also take private referrals, but before you take this step carefully check the voluntary organization's internal procedures (which might forbid you from doing this). Also check the procedures to see what happens after you leave the voluntary organization as you may wish to contact the referring agency again. You are strongly advised to discuss this in supervision and with the management of the organization.

Supervision

After you have found your supervisor one of the things that you can discuss is where to find clients. As your work together proceeds, your supervisor will build confidence in your practice and might begin to refer clients to you whom he or she cannot take. Supervisors are also often a good source of local knowledge and contacts.

Indirect marketing

Whilst this is the last on my list of marketing strategies in fact I think that it is probably one of the best ways to raise your profile as a counsellor or therapist. By indirect marketing I mean offering talks, training workshops, supervision or other forms of activities in your locality. These activities could be with counselling organizations, mental health or nursing groups, medical groups, health visitors, homemakers, teachers, etc. You will have to be either an expert on something or become an expert on something through reading and further training. Creative thinking about what to offer can often bring rewards, for example, talks to teachers on anger management including providing an understanding of transference to help teachers think about what might be happening with difficult pupils.

Some doubts about advertising

Having dealt with the practicalities of advertising, I want to plant one or two doubts in your mind. Traditionally counsellors and psychotherapists have not advertised, and it is only relatively

Table 3.1 Trends in advertising in the BACP journal

Date of BACP journal	Number of adverts for day conferences/ seminars	Number of adverts for training courses	Number of adverts for publications	Number of adverts for therapy rooms to let	Number of adverts for counselling/ supervision
February 1986	2	1	2	0	0
February 1996	21	59	2	1	7
February 2006	27	51	1	15	56

Note: the size of adverts has been ignored for this analysis; only the number has been counted.

recently that psychotherapists seem to have started. The feeling in the profession until now appears to have been that clients will find their way to a therapist if they need one. The counter-argument is that potential clients do not know how to find a therapist and indeed the low level of public awareness of what counselling and therapy can offer is partly to blame for this lack of public profile for the profession. Alongside this, it can also be argued that in a society where advertising is part and parcel of everyday life, adverts from psychotherapists and counsellors might no longer be out of place. Table 3.1 provides an analysis of trends in advertising in the BACP journal over the past 20 years.

It is interesting to note that in the February 1986 edition of the journal there were no advertisements for counselling or supervision (and a very small number for training, conferences and books). By February 1996 the number for training and books had risen significantly and there were a small number (seven adverts) for counselling/supervision. Ten years later (February 2006) there were significantly more adverts for training, conferences and rooms to let and 56 adverts for supervision/counselling. The table speaks for itself and suggests that within the profession colleague-to-colleague attitudes towards advertising have changed significantly over the last 20 years and more particularly over the last decade.

It is not entirely clear why the professions of counselling and psychotherapy developed the attitude of reluctance and suspicion towards more public advertising. My hunch is that it stems from the history of psychoanalysis and its close links to the medical profession, with the latter's particular set of ethics and attitudes in relation to advertising. It is therefore worth looking briefly at the history and debate within the medical profession over advertising and promotion as this may throw light on our own attitudes and practice.

Irvine (1991) provides a thorough survey of the history of advertising of doctors' services within the UK, including the external (legal) and internal General Medical Council (GMC) and British Medical Association (BMA) debates. In 1905 the BMA asked the GMC to issue 'a warning notice to medical practitioners against the practice of canvassing and advertising for the procuring of patients' (Irvine 1991: 35). There followed a general ban on all advertising for doctors (but curiously not for dentists who were also covered by the GMC at that stage). The London Psycho-analytic Society was established in 1913, to become the British Psycho-analytic Society in 1919. Initially its membership comprised only medical practitioners and it is not difficult to imagine that they brought with them the prevailing attitudes within the medical profession towards advertising of services. Even today the Institute of Psychoanalysis (the training body for the BP-AS founded in 1924) emphasizes the medical background of its applicants:

> The Institute of Psychoanalysis welcomes applicants . . . Many students are psychiatrists or medically qualified, some are child or adult psychotherapists, psychologists, social workers or academics, and some come from another background altogether.
>
> (BP-AS website March 2006)

During the early 1980s, with changing attitudes by doctors and the general public towards advertising, the total prohibition on advertising began to make less sense for both doctors and patients. In 1984 the Patients Liaison Group of the Royal College of General Practitioners published a paper arguing for better general information for patients. This resulted in a loosening of the strictures of the 1905 code, allowing some dissemination of basic information via Citizens Advice Bureau (CAB) offices, townhalls, libraries and the like, but still forbidding promotional advertising. This was very shortly overtaken in 1986 by the interest of the Office of Fair Trading (OFT) which had responsibility for identifying unfair or anticompetitive practice. As a result of a detailed inquiry undertaken on behalf of the OFT by the Monopolies and Mergers Commission, a new policy emerged which distinguished between 'the ethical dissemination of relevant factual information' (GMC 1987) and three more contentious areas of promotional advertising, canvassing or touting, and disparagement of professional colleagues (Irvine 1991: 38). The GMC recognized that distinguishing between information giving and promotional advertising required a subjective judgement and so the GMC moved to a procedure whereby they provided specific instructions on what might be included in literature and thereby relaxed controls over how this information might be distributed.

This brings us to the current policies of the BMA and GMC. As recently as 1989 the BMA reaffirmed its opposition to advertising: 'That the Association, while recognising the need to inform patients about medical services, strongly opposes advertising by doctors' (BMA website March 2006). The GMC adopted a revised third edition Code of Good Medical Practice in May 2001 which is remarkably similar to that currently operated by the UKCP. Basically the information should be factual, verifiable, conform to the law, make no claims of cure and must not play on patients' fears in order to get them to sign up (GMC 2001).

It is curious that although the medical traditions in Britain and the USA have been quite different in terms of public and private medicine, the attitudes towards advertising have been remarkably similar with parallel developments. In the USA advertising by doctors was almost non-existent until the late 1970s (Lober 1993), with the overwhelming number of physicians opposed to advertising (Folland et al. 1989), despite the clear financial gain it could bring to practices. In the UK, although medicine is predominantly publicly funded, each GP is in a sense a self-employed practitioner whose income depends on the size of their patient list and the number of special procedures they might undertake. In this respect there is surprising similarity between doctors in the UK and USA in terms of how they earn their income. In the USA there was also an anti-trust investigation over restraint of trade through the ban on advertising and in 1979 the Federal Trade Commission declared that the American Medical Association was in breach of the law. The case ended in the Supreme Court where, in 1982, the court ruled in favour of the FTC.

The parallels between developments and thinking within the medical profession in the USA and Britain on the question of advertising by practitioners, and how and why it might be controlled, appear to have been mirrored by UK psychotherapy and counselling organizations to the point where the GMC and UKCP codes are now remarkably similar.

In his abstract, Irvine states: 'Medicine is unique amongst professions and trades, offering a "product" which is unlike any other' (1991: 35). This claim is not wholly true as counsellors and psychotherapists are also offering a relationship-based intervention leading to the better well-being and mental health of the client. However, the stress on the word 'product' is important as for therapists it serves to underline the centrality of the therapeutic relationship in what is offered.

For some counsellors and psychotherapists, it may not matter to them how much they allow their clients to know about them before the work starts. However, if you work from a theoretical model where it is important for the client to create their own projected image of you, then you might need to think more carefully about what you use in your advertising. I have in mind those who work more from a psychodynamic or psychoanalytic perspective.

It is a debatable issue about how much clients get to know about their therapist once the work begins: for example, from the room in which the therapist works, or the way they dress, their accent, choice of vocabulary, or, of more complexity, the unconscious clues the therapist gives to the client's unconscious. It is easy to imagine that unconscious communication is one-way traffic (from patient to therapist), but this is missing a significant point about the patient's unconscious ability to tune in to their therapist. Not every patient will be able to bring this knowledge into their awareness (much to the relief of many therapists), so to some extent we may feel protected. However if this information now lies in the patient's unconscious they may feel an unconscious pressure to act on it.

The issue gets a little more complicated. Many therapists, including psychoanalytic psychotherapists, publish books or articles in newspapers. Whilst few patients will read the more learned journals in the hope of finding out something about their therapist (that is except other therapists who are also patients), books and newspapers are open for all to read. Whilst these publications are not advertising per se, they do convey a wealth of information about the writer to the potential client, and probably very much more than a webpage. But as far as I know no one would suggest that the profession should stop publishing.

Kupers (1986), in his discussion of the dual potential for brief therapy, highlights the potential unleashed by models of brief therapy in making mental health provision more available and equitable. However, he goes on to argue that 'this potentiality can be turned into its opposite' (p. 95) by reinforcing the double standard of the wealthy still being able to afford long-term therapy and the poor frequently remaining on long waiting lists for a six-session intervention which is symptom focused rather than about personal growth. In short, drawing on Marcuse, his argument is that with every advance in society there follows a repression in order to defuse the development of its liberating or subversive qualities.

I would like to develop this idea by way of an analogy which focuses on the effects on the relationship between providers and users when the providers make apparently helpful changes to the context of that relationship. A number of years ago I was struck by the fact that the successors to British Rail stopped using the term 'passengers' and started using 'customers' instead. This was a move very much in keeping with the development of the consumer society and no doubt designed in part to make the 'customers' feel better about delays and late trains. The potential of the new name, where we move from passive passengers to active customers, implies greater involvement by the customers in choice and the hope that we will be treated differently (i.e. better). In practice the move has made little or no difference to the service: there is not greater choice but in fact greater confusion over ticket prices, less flexibility in using tickets on competing rail providers, and so on. Expectations were raised by the change to 'customers' and then dashed, making matters worse.

In the same vein, therapists need to consider the consequences on the therapeutic relationship of a move to a more open practice of advertising our offerings. On the one hand it is probably agreed that advertising will make members of the public more aware of our names and that we offer something called counselling or psychotherapy. The result could be that more people seek our services and so begin to feel better. To this extent advertising could be seen as a liberating move.

However, our adverts do little towards actually educating the public of the value of what we offer and I fear it could be worse

than that. In an increasingly consumerist society where the con-
sumers are encouraged to seek out the best bargain or the quickest
fixes, our advertisements run the risk of reinforcing rather than
challenging these values. Like the railways, adverts imply customers rather than patients/clients, thus potentially changing the
nature of our relationship with clients. Are we going to be expected
to be experts in technique or delivering a 'cure' at the expense of
exploring a creative, unfolding relationship? Perhaps this is not an
issue for therapists who work solely in brief focused models, but for
those who prefer working within an interpersonal or intersubjective
model, it has to be an issue.

Stavkakakis (2000) reminds us of the media's attitude towards
therapy when he quotes from a review by Dylan Evans in *The
Guardian*:

> The word 'industry' is appropriate, since psychotherapy now
> wields all the tools of a successful trade, replete with devious
> marketing strategies, political support, and a sophisticated
> 'technology of victim making'. In order to survive therapists
> need patients, which they 'create' by labelling every quirk of
> personality a 'disorder'. The potential for therapy becomes the
> whole world.
>
> (p. 34)

Whatever our reaction to the above quotation, there can be no
doubt that every move towards wholesale advertising pushed us
towards an industry of the sort described. Far from liberating the
public from their ignorance of what we offer, we might in fact be
selling them a version of therapy that is either consumerist or falls
into the trap suggested in the quotation, with the result that the
therapeutic relationship as we know it is seriously eroded.

So it is not just a case of caveat emptor, buyer beware, it is also
a case of seller beware as our collective efforts to gain clients
through publicity could be argued to threaten the very thing we
hold in high regard – the therapeutic relationship.

References

British Association for Counselling (1986) *Counselling* 15, February.
British Association for Counselling (1996) *Counselling* 7(1).
British Association for Counselling and Psychotherapy (2002) *Ethical*

Framework for Good Practice in Counselling and Psychotherapy, Rugby: BACP.

British Association for Counselling and Psychotherapy (2006) *Therapy* 17(1).

Clark, J. (2002) *Freelance Counselling and Psychotherapy: Competition and Collaboration*, London: Routledge.

Folland, S., Parameswaran, R. and Darling, J. (1989) On the nature of physicians' opposition to advertising, *Journal of Advertising* 18(1): 4–9.

General Medical Council (1987) *Professional Conduct and Discipline: Fitness to Practice*, London: GMC.

General Medical Council (2001) *Good Medical Practice*, 3rd edn, London: GMC.

Irvine, D. H. (1991) The advertising of doctors' services, *Journal of Medical Ethics* 17: 35–40.

Jenkins, P. (2004) *Access to Records of Counselling and Psychotherapy*, Rugby: BACP.

Lober, C. W. (1993) Physician advertising, *Dermatologic Clinics* 11(2): 281–284.

Kupers, T. A. (1986) The dual potential of brief psychotherapy, Free Associations.

Roth, A. and Fonagy, P. (1996) *What Works for Whom? A Critical Review of Psychotherapy Research*, New York: Guilford Press.

Stavkakakis, T. (2000) The ethics of psychoanalysis: a Lacanian perpective, in J. Raphael-Leff (ed.) *Ethics of Psychoanalysis*, Colchester: Centre for Psychoanalytic Studies, University of Essex.

Thistle, R. (1998) *Counselling and Psychotherapy in Private Practice*, London: Sage.

Webpages

British Association for Counselling and Psychotherapy (2005) Advertising policy. [Online] Rugby: BACP. Available from: http://www.bacp.co.uk/join_bacp/advertising_policy.html (15 March 2006).

British Medical Association (2004) Guidance from the Ethics Department February 2004: Advertising. [Online] London: BMA. Available from: http://www.bma.org.uk/ap.nsf/Content/NHSprivate~Advertising?Open Document&Highlight=2,advertising (15 March 2006).

British Psychoanalytic Society (2005) Homepage. [Online] London: BPS. Available from: http://www.psychoanalysis.org.uk/frontpage.htm (15 March 2006).

United Kingdom Council for Psychotherapy (2002) The internet and advertising. [Online] London: UKCP. Available from: http://www.psychotherapy.org.uk/ukcp_advertising.html (15 March 2006).

Chapter 4

Assessment

Melanie Withers

> Naturally things cannot in reality fit together the way the
> evidence does in my letter, life is more than a Chinese puzzle.
> (Franz Kafka, letter to his father)

Introduction

> Laura arrives, a small woman sitting in the waiting area. She is neatly
> dressed, in her early thirties with dark hair and an expectant look on
> her face. As she sits down she comments on the décor of the
> consulting room. Who is assessing whom?

Generally any new social encounter involves a mutual scrutiny. It
is not surprising then that psychotherapy or counselling[1] should
use the assessment interview as the starting point for a therapeutic
relationship (Tantam 1995). However, in private practice client
'choice' suggests that this process has far greater challenges than
those posed for the therapist working within a statutory service.
No longer does the hapless client persuade a busy practitioner to
take on their 'case'. They may still wish to prove they are worthy
of the therapist's time, but here our client has actual purchasing
power with attendant ability to shop around – and crucially to
assess not just trustworthiness but desirability of the therapist as
partner in the whole enterprise.

The 1990s saw the rise of the employee assistance programmes
(EAPs) posing further challenges to what had been slow and
steady, open-ended, bread and butter work. Practitioners now
found themselves required to see clients for five sessions or so and
moreover demonstrate some kind of effective shift in the client's

psyche or functioning during that time. Work was to be focused and solution orientated. The relationship between purchaser and provider was by now even more firmly established in the public mind. Arguably, any therapist could opt to decline, stating a desire to remain true to their original training, but in a competitive field few but the most established could afford to take the risk of remaining so therapeutically purist.

Additionally, the previous decade saw unprecedented numbers of graduate counsellors and therapists dispensed from their training institution on to an unsuspecting public – bringing maybe a freshness of approach and a greater range of techniques, but also a willingness to undercut the market in order to gain experience necessary for professional registration. The impact of therapy research, attempts to decide what works for whom (Roth and Fonagy 1996) and the appearance of 'evidence based' concepts (Rowland and Goss 2000) have also called into question existing practice, sending the first twinges of postmodern anxiety to therapists' chairs around the country.

> Laura begins to talk about the reasons why she is seeking help. She has been in a relationship for five years with her partner and is beginning to have real doubts about whether he is the 'one' for her. Her anxiety is becoming overwhelming, she has panic attacks and she is drinking more than she would like. She is a history teacher, working in a secondary school, where she is terrified someone will find out she is not coping. She has no children of her own and wonders if she should stay with her current partner and have a child – or leave?
>
> Whilst taking note of the panic symptoms (CBT?) relationship problems (psychodynamic therapy?) and desire to resolve her dilemma (solution-focused therapy?) the assessor also observes that she is attractive – and that she has a secure job.

Naturally any therapist must be able to begin the therapeutic process by investigating the client's world, both internally and externally, past and present (Holmes 1995), though the details vary according to the therapeutic model employed and a cognitive behavioural assessment, for example, would look at different features (Zindel *et al.* 1995). However constructed, these have important implications for therapeutic relating, safety, ethical practice and ultimately the progress and outcome of the therapy itself.

Private practice offers a particular freedom to take on those who are not suited to the therapy offered by the state sector. Often chronically short of cash, the NHS and other statutory services are constantly trying to manage meagre resources. As a result, therapy offered may be time limited, or it may be restricted in other ways, providing a limited range of therapeutic approaches, for example. Research evidence too, though helpful, is measuring what serves the greater good and may not be appropriate at micro level. As we know, the one size fits all policy raises difficult questions for those who do not fit. Where private practice scores each time is in having greater flexibility to treat the client individually, thereby offering a highly targeted and confidential service tailored to the specific choices, details and dilemmas with which each client presents.

However, these positive attributes conceal a shadow. To maintain a private practice the therapist must also understand market forces, including those related to his or her own capacity to attract and retain clients as well as the numbers and complexity of cases which can effectively be managed at any one time.[2] As the first port of call, assessment in the private sector, while attempting to be the most objective of interviews, is at once the most vulnerable to mutually seductive and even delusional thinking unless the therapist's needs to remain solvent and the client's financial potency can be acknowledged.

For the client, the notion of choice brings with it far greater scope to demand practical arrangements, negotiate terms, request a particular mode of therapy or particular kind of therapist. Whilst some of this may be reasonable, and brings a reminder of adult-to-adult relating into what can become an infantilizing and disempowering process for the client, it has the disadvantage of feeding a fantasy that the ultimate parent, endlessly attuned to one's needs, can both be found and purchased.

For the therapist, decisions made via the assessment process may look as if they are based solely on experienced clinical judgement. However, it is inevitable that the fundamental financial dynamic at the heart of private work suggest that these will contain unconscious invitations to collude and anxieties about how much may be confronted. Tantam (1995), for example, claims the initial interview provides much needed hope for the distressed client. Although offering relief and maybe containing the client's anxiety, this has a worrying dimension that is hard to substantiate should the subsequent sessions fail to deliver, and arguably leaves the private practitioner vulnerable to accusations of misrepresentation.

Some authors, namely Syme (1994), claim that supervision can be a way of exploring the ethical position that the assessor may be pushed into but, as Teitlebaum (1990) counters, the supervisor's own blind spots can intervene. Here a shared understanding on the need to remain solvent and possible unconscious envy, to name but two, make any supervisor's own position open to scrutiny. Positioned thus as both expert by client need and potential seducer by his or her own, the therapist's subscription to Freud's rule of abstinence (1915) becomes particularly challenging at this point.

Why assess: diagnosis or assessment?

It could be argued that there is no need for assessment in private practice as, unlike statutory or agency work, the therapist tends to be assessing those clients whom he or she will continue to see. Provided too that satisfactory mutual terms can be negotiated, no case need be made via a third party such as an NHS department for the green light go ahead. Therefore diagnostic ideas which might aim to explore disease through symptoms and will also have to come up with some kind of treatment plan have less impact in private work. Theoretically then, once initial contact is made both parties may move straight to therapy. However, having a clear theory of what one is offering and why is one way of managing the potential for mutual exploitation hazarded above. So although a treatment strategy need not be decided upon for resource management issues as in agency work, in some branches of therapeutic practice there is considerable pressure on the therapist to formulate one in the interests of appearing professional and behaving ethically.

Purpose

Despite the medical backdrop to diagnosis as a concept, Tyndale (1998) maintains that although this and assessment are double tasks in therapy, deciding whether or not a client can use the treatment on offer is perfectly possible provided one is also aware of relational concepts. A trawl through the relevant literature reveals several claims supporting this. Etchegoyen (1991) stresses the importance of the interpersonal aspects and Ogden (1989) feels it is problematic to take on those we dislike despite analysing our own negative transference. Holmes (1995) describes the helpfulness of assessment as a forerunner to therapy proper in terms of looking for diagnosis, treatability and prognosis. He describes two features: the chance to grasp the client's predicament empathically and to calculate the likelihood of therapeutic success. For Tantam (1995) it offers the opportunity to gather information and gives a taste of the treatment. Coltart (1993) looks for 'psychological mindedness' and several mention 'transference readiness' and 'degree of motivation' as factors to look for associated with successful outcome.

Hinshelwood (1995) looks for the site of maximum pain and uses trial interpretations to explore how well the client manages the process. Holmes (1995) sees the assessment interview as a session in its own right and as Rycroft (1995) points out, some clients may be simply misinformed about therapy. What they really need, he says, is a neurologist or a good divorce lawyer and the assessment interview is then both first and last meeting. For Ogden (1989) however, the initial meeting must be seen as the beginning of the therapeutic process itself and not just the preparation for it.[3] Many authors mention harm minimization (Mace 1995) although it is important to remember that there can never be such a thing as zero risk care (Maynard 2000).

For the client entering treatment there is considerable investment in terms of time and money as well as the possibility of being caught up in traumatic feelings or finding the experience actively damaging. For the therapist it may feel frightening to carry the potential risk to the client in what amounts to an outpatient setting, especially if there are mental health concerns. Second, it can be frightening at a personal level. Apart from the obvious risk involved in meeting a (disturbed?) stranger for the first time, it is important to assess the potential for therapeutic improvement. A lengthy therapy where little progress is made or which contains overwhelming painful features can be thoroughly demoralizing if not unbearable for the therapist (Berkwitz 1998).

Prediction

What is less clear is how much of this can be foreseen in advance. Malan (1979) using a quasi-medico language of indication and contra-indication suggested that by using his two triangles of the person and of defences an assessment interview should be able to pick up the essential details of the client's life and furthermore predict the likely outcome of therapy during the treatment period. Several authors have tried to tackle this head-on using their preferred model of therapy as a guide to expand and explore Malan's proposition.

Some focus on the interpersonal dynamics. Hinshelwood (1995) constructs an argument in favour of psychodynamic formulation – a series of hypotheses to be tried out on the patient much akin to the process of therapy itself. He bases his thinking on the client's description about their current situation – often the reason for seeking therapy – and tracks this against what is known about early object relations and speculates as to how this is likely to be played out in the transference. Fonagy (in Klein 1999) adapts the Adult Attachment Interview to explore the client's capacity for reflective functioning. He suggests that by listening to people in a systematic way it is possible to predict the strength and nature of their defences against understanding themselves and those around them – including their prospective therapist – which will give some indication as to how therapy may pan out.

Some focus on the narrative. Davis (1998) takes the idea that the client's story can be read like a text on many levels: manifest, contextual and interactional. The assessment interview represents the beginnings of a decoding process where the client's material reveals unconscious communication that requires translating in the context of a therapeutic relationship. The unconscious of both client and therapist is involved in a mutual dialogue. Reformulation of the problem is key and recommendations for treatment are to be made on that basis.

Some focus on the intrapsychic. Kernberg, according to Klein (1999), looks for three features: first, ego strength, including levels of impulse control, tolerance of anxiety and frustration; second, identity confusion and awareness of the boundaries between self and other; third, the degree of reality-based awareness. Recommendations are made for future work on the extent to which these categories are present or absent. Similar claims to predictive understanding can be found in the literature of the Cognitive Behavioural, Cognitive Analytic and Humanistic therapies (Mace 1995).

As all of the above could be applied to most clients, it would seem that what the authors are picking up is severity of disturbance. All are trying to assess initial degrees of damage and psychic robustness following the old adage of selecting the client for treatment who is 'sick enough to need it and healthy enough to stand it'. Consideration of these features, according to the model employed, is then used to recommend a particular kind of therapy to the client. This may vary from intensive psychoanalysis to supportive counselling and, in some instances, no therapy at all.

However, it is by no means obvious how assessment conclusions predict what should or could happen next. What we are left with is a set of ideas which arguably do not map on to any greater certainty than a theoretical one, which may or may not inform the therapist of the nature of the client's problem, and may or may not help him or her to know what to do next. It is also clear, if one pays heed to Bion's famous request that we approach every session without memory and desire, that too much attention paid to initial formulations can close down the possibility of the new and the unknown unknowability which needs to arise if transformation is to happen (Ogden 1989; Denman 1995).

Additionally, there are strong suspicions from reading the literature that therapists then recommend that approach in which they themselves have been trained as being the preferred option (Klein 1999). So it could be argued that the outcome is a foregone conclusion anyway. Assessing is seen as something which requires seniority and skill based on substantial clinical experience and for both client and therapist there are strong forces at work which reinforce belief in therapist expertise. One has to have a notion of authority, either internally or externally constructed, in order to speak and therapist transference to their own organizations is legion within the profession. For the therapist in private practice, material provided during assessments, even if at heart representing only theoretical speculations, remains a crucial link to their professional colleagues. Relatively isolated compared with those working in agency settings, private practitioners need to adhere to a body of knowledge often provided by their training organization to manage their own anxieties around potential harm to the client or themselves. Yet if this all comes down to subjective judgements rather than objective overview, on the surface this might appear worryingly imprecise.

Therapeutic expertise

Throughout this chapter there remains a conflict of terms which always threatens to overwhelm the points under discussion and this lies at the very heart of the assessor's dilemma. Therapy is in a state of confusion precisely because of the multiple claims on its identity. Unlike the medical world there are few certainties as to the origins of client distress as the theories outlined above illustrate via their comprehensive but conflicting ideas of what is important. Freud and his followers, especially in the Anglo-Saxon world, attempted to turn psychoanalysis into a science in order to give it credibility, and therapists have been forced to borrow heavily from medical terminology ever since. The various DSM manuals and other measures of symptom identification continue to illustrate the therapeutic community's anxiety for evidence to support subjective judgements and to turn them into something which looks more clinically respectable.

Some attempts have been made to utilize this in assessment, specifically with the Clinical Outcomes in Routine Evaluation (CORE) system (CORE 1998). Pioneered by Leeds University and used widely in the NHS and other clinical settings which gives it a statistical benchmarking relevance, the system is a subjective measure of distress where clients are invited to complete a pre- and post-therapy questionnaire. The aim is to show that disturbance reduces as a result of therapy and can be useful to measure change – although as always, valid criticisms can be levied at any measure which seeks to categorize human experience into number crunching. As J. Klein (1999) comments:

> From the beginnings of psychoanalysis, we have resorted to diagnostic-sounding categories such as depression, obsessional states, anxiety states. Unlike medical diseases, however, these are states of the mind. They have no secure etiologies, nor reliable prognoses, nor have we reliable therapeutics. There is very little which says we should treat borderline personalities in one way, hysterics in another. And so on.
>
> (p. 334)

Clinical data leading to the development of 'evidence based practice' (Rowland and Goss 2000) have added to the debate. Meanwhile academic influences in the form of psychology departments have attempted to look at efficacy and outcome in order to demonstrate scientific status. Some have even built computer models of the factors determining assessment decisions and treatment recommendations (Birtle and Buckingham 1995). No wonder the assessor is pressured into making what sound like authoritative pronouncements as to what is wrong and how to fix it. As Lees (1998) points out, the research evidence alongside the clinical perspective gives the impression of even more conflict, polarization and fragmentation.

However, more worrying still is the concept of clinical conclusions in themselves. In a postmodern world a notion of separate identity, as has been assumed for so long, is called into question. Post-Freudian developments look at the psychic relationships between people rather than individual autonomous behaviour and problems of an internal world (Elliot 1994). Distress cannot be traced only to sexual repression or untrammelled desire, but is seen contextually as the result of disturbed relationships. Parker *et al.* (1995) have tracked madness as a culturally constructed phenomenon where images of madness and normality are woven into the language we use. By deconstructing clinical categories and noting the oppositional forces at work it becomes clear that society is using the concept of 'difference' to regulate that which it wishes to repudiate. By locating madness in an 'other' – the individual – society is able to abdicate responsibility. But if the individual exists only against the background of society, the concept of 'otherness' collapses and the individual becomes one and the same with that which he or she most wishes to disavow. Subjective experience becomes intersubjective.

Therapeutic judgements

Freud's concepts of the neurotic, perverse or psychotic as taken up by Lacan (Fink 1997) have only a very loose relationship to psychiatric literature, though continuing to borrow heavily from the medical model. Lacan, as a psychiatrist, felt that personality was ordered by one of these three categories and that this was a fixed state. At assessment it is therefore vital to determine which one and a proper diagnosis is needed. Otherwise to offer a talking treatment to someone psychotically structured and therefore presenting with borderline features was possibly hazardous and probably a waste of time. But states of mind cannot be isolated like bacteria and Freud's research methodology was confined to case studies. What remains awry here is that the medical and the therapeutic models are employing different language games. If one applies the rules of one to the other the danger is that one only comes up with nonsense. At times it is important to salvage baby whilst maybe dispensing with bathwater, and for some the medical model will continue to be the most appropriate response.

> Mark is 42 with a long psychiatric history. A mature student at university he has not been hospitalised for six years. He meets some stress around hand-in dates and goes to the university counselling centre where he is encouraged to come off his medication for reasons that are not clear. After therapy finishes he begins to have a return of his auditory hallucinations and consults a private therapist.
>
> The assessor's conclusion based on sitting with Mark for an hour is that he has been coping well, suggests further therapy may not help and recommends he go back on his medication. She says he is welcome to return if there is anything he feels he wants to talk about, but he says he only wants the voices to stop.

Psychoanalytic practice appears to have evolved through personal analysis, self-reflection and a reviewing of technique in the light of both of these. What seems clear from clinical work is that clients can move in and out of hysteric, borderline and obsessional states, which might be better construed as positions, and that crisis, levels of desperation or anxiety amongst other criteria are key features in the process. One can no longer think of a hysteric or an obsessive as Freud wished to believe, as these positions are present, at least potentially, in all of us.

Additionally, most clinicians know that there are those clients who at assessment might not appear to fit the conventional criteria for a talking treatment. Maybe they exhibit too many borderline, hysteric, ambivalent or resistant characteristics, but it is important to remember that assessment offers only a momentary clinical snapshot of someone in relation to the someone of the assessor, rather than a comprehensive diagnostic picture. One should never underestimate the place of anxiety in a first meeting. There are those who are taken on and subsequently benefit greatly. It is therapist subjective judgements rather than adherence to a model that helps decide which.

> Alex is 25 and also has a psychiatric history with suicidal and self-harming ideation. She arrives distressed and behaves in ways that

suggests clear borderline tendencies in the initial interview. However at assessment it becomes clear that she has a great deal that she wishes to talk about, her mother's abandonment of her as a child, her difficult relationship and her determination to find other ways of managing her distress. The assessor is concerned, but feels there is sufficient client robustness (and psychiatric safety measures in place) to commence therapy. Moreover in exploring her countertransference to Alex she feels optimistic. From such unprepossessing beginnings it goes well

It is clear to see that the risks are great, especially in taking such clients into private therapy, and that decisions based on experiential understanding and relational fit are worrying for a community with an uneasy sense of its clinical authority, dealing with severe levels of human distress. But at its very heart and in its very origins therapy is a subjective process – albeit a shared one – and the task within the therapeutic community is not to continuously deny this but to make it acceptable.[4]

Assessing the client

It is now proposed to look further at the original client with which this chapter commenced and to discuss some hypotheses about what is behind her anxiety and what emerges with the assessor who conducts the initial meeting:

Laura is the third child of older parents. She thinks of herself as the afterthought as her next sibling was 13 when she was born. She feels she is surrounded by approaching loss. Her eldest brother has haemophilia and subsequently contracted HIV. Her older sister's children are both haemophiliac, though Laura herself is not a carrier.

She has not told her mother who is 73 and going blind how she feels, as the relationship though affectionate has always been a remote one. Both parents were wrapped up in each other to the exclusion of their children. Her father is a retired academic who was equally distant when she was growing up and she feels she was brought up as much by her sister as by her parents. The family moved around fairly often when she was young because of her father's job and she went to several schools – feeling unable to establish longlasting relationships after a while. 'There was little point in saying I would keep in touch – it always petered out after a few years.'

Her work at the school is particularly stressful. As a more experienced teacher she has been given additional pastoral responsibility and finds this almost impossible to manage. She feels she cannot take on any more of other people's problems. The final straw came with the birth of her partner's sister's baby a few months ago. The child is confirmed as having special needs. It is this she thinks that has triggered her panic symptoms and brought her to the point of collapse.

The factors shown in Figure 4.1 represent areas for potential exploration and suggest some possible narrative routes which might be helpful in getting to know Laura and deciding whether or not to offer her therapy.

1 Presenting problem

Laura is suffering from anxiety both at home and at work. There is some urgency to all of this and she feels the situation is getting worse. The problem has been going on for six weeks, focused on the birth of her partner's sister's child. She is able to function at work still though with some difficulty, dresses carefully and seems both desperate and keen.

The assessor notes that she is not at the point of disintegration and her expectancy suggests motivation. She also realizes this is the kind of client with whom she has worked successfully in the past. The problems are acute but not chronic, began fairly recently and seem clearly related to a reactive crisis rather than a more severe internalized difficulty. The new baby's birth represents a clear 'why now?' Is her anxiety related to a fear that she has unconsciously damaged the baby out of envy? If so, is she afraid of Oedipal potency?

2 Relationships and support

She says her partner is very supportive and cannot understand why she feels so ambivalent about the relationship. They had always

---

1 Presenting symptoms or problems
- What is the presenting issue: severity, length of onset, narrative dimension, degree of attached demand, motivation for change?
- Why now?

2 Relationships and support
- What is the quality of the client's ability to make relationships or not?
- What is the family history?
- Attachment patterns?
- Has she or he enough internal or external support to cope with the therapeutic process?

3 Insight
- How much use can the client make of a talking treatment?
- How does the client experience and understand their difficulties?

4 Affect
- Are emotions latent or manifest?
- Does she or he have psychosomatic symptoms?

5 Family, social and cultural issues
- Are these such as to contraindicate counselling or therapy?
- Are there issues to do with race, gender, sexual orientation or disability?
- How old is the client?

6 Medical or psychiatric history
- Is the client on medication (including illegal drugs or alcohol)?
- Has she or he previously been seen by the psychiatric services?
- Are there previous psychiatric or medical diagnoses that might contraindicate therapy?

7 Therapeutic alliance
- Is there enough therapist–client rapport to allow a therapeutic exploration?
- Is she or he psychologically minded?
- Transference readiness?
- Has she or he had therapy before?
- If the work is time limited, can a focus be identified?

8 Practical questions
- Does the client have a particular adherence to a model?
- Is this realistic?
- Are there boundary problems?
- Time concerns?
- Who is paying?
- Can therapy proceed with safety?
- Is disability a practical issue?
- What is the state of current waiting lists?
- Is it possible/desirable to refer on to another agency or therapist if necessary or appropriate?

Figure 4.1 Factors in the assessment of clients influencing referral and treatment options

planned to have children one day. However her early life reflects a pattern of isolation and loss, with parents who were not altogether interested in her and school friends who were endlessly left behind. There is also a morbid quality to this family and Laura seems much preoccupied with imminent death of one or other family member.

The assessor hypothesizes that Laura has the capacity to make relationships and so falls into the post-Oedipal or three-person relating group who have mastered basic attachment. She is well supported so that insights of therapy are unlikely to leave her lonely and overwhelmed. The assessor wonders if the endless losses in childhood are what lie behind her difficulty in really committing to a long-term relationship with her partner. She notes the loss and how Laura seems consumed by fear of further death and tragedy in the family. How might this affect the therapeutic relationship? Additionally, she wonders if Laura fears either any child she were to have would be taken away, or conversely could the birth of a healthy child be experienced as attacking by a family where there is so much ill health?

3 Insight

Laura responds well to a linking statement that maybe it is difficult working with the children at school when those in her family are all so sick. However, she has little idea about what is making her so anxious except that what has happened to the baby is so awful. She then describes in detail her butterfly stomach and shivery shoulders.

The assessor feels she is able to reflect on what is happening, but has areas which she quickly defends at assessment at least preventing much insight. Laura is retreating into panic symptoms to mask perhaps her rage that her partner's family is showing signs of being as sick as her own?

4 Affect

Laura becomes tearful quite quickly especially when talking about her lonely childhood, but then excuses her parents from blame.

The assessor wonders about rage again and why there are no signs of it? Maybe it is difficult to get angry with an elderly mother when there is little time left, or a father with whom time is so precious anyway?

5 Family, social and cultural issues

> Laura is white British, as is the assessor. She is 32. Her brother has had some therapy, which did not help.

There appear to be no cultural aspects which might contra-indicate therapy, though family pessimism might get in the way. The assessor notes the ethnic and cultural similarities and considers how this might lead to assumptions being made between her and the client which could go overlooked. Further, she wonders about Laura's biological clock as a further 'why now?', but otherwise developmentally she is on the cusp of a shift which suggests she is ripe for therapeutic intervention.

6 Medical or psychiatric history

> Laura copes via self-medication, dosing herself up on white wine each night. She has been to her GP and is currently on beta blockers for her anxiety. There is no psychiatric history.

The assessor notices the self-sufficiency of Laura's coping strategies and wonders how typical this might be for a child brought up in relative isolation. She wonders if her drinking could become problematic, but also notes that Laura is not so addicted to wine that she is not also looking for other sources of help.

7 Therapeutic alliance

> Laura is an attractive looking and thoughtful woman. She responds well to the suggestion that she has been through a lot recently and might like someone to take it all away. She is able to speculate on less contentious issues, including her sense that she does not seek support at school because her schooling was always about 'getting on with it'.

This could be evidence of psychological mindedness. The assessor notices the need and the transferential invitation for a maternal figure. She responds to Laura's distress and vulnerability and is aware of corresponding warmth as well as identification with some aspects of Laura's story. She notes a strong desire to suggest Laura takes time off work – maybe a sign that the therapeutic relationship is a passable 'fit' so far? But she also notes some anxiety and awkwardness in her own countertransference as Laura leaves the room at the end of the interview. Did this represent her projective unconscious anxiety that she was a nuisance as maybe she had felt with her mother?

8 Practical questions

Laura wants once weekly therapy. She is able to pay the stated fee. When asked how long she feels this will take she says she thinks about six months.

The assessor notes the time limit and that this is not going to be a thorough analysis of everything that is potentially troubling Laura. She notes Laura's adult way of negotiating the terms and despite the regressive invitation (childhood loneliness) feels that the frequency most probably suits the therapeutic task as stated. The assessor decides that this is a client who is likely to benefit from a talking treatment, but is aware once more of the shadow. Maybe Laura wants to bypass a deeper therapeutic commitment as, hypothetically, she might be doing in her other relationships. Is she frightened to get close for fear of further loss and disappointment? In which case the relatively brief contract is less a sign of health and rather more one of avoidance or even challenge to the therapist to be proactive in ways that the parents could not. One could go on speculating as it is only in the therapy itself that any of this will become valid, illusory or just plain wrong.

9 Discussion

Finally what remain interesting are those areas less hard to define. Why was it that this client came and spoke to a female therapist only a few years older than herself and the focus turned to children? Was it projection, clinical need, avoidance of other matters or that somehow the assessor was pulled into paying more attention to those features herself? Might not another therapist have focused more on the performative or work-related aspects of the client's narrative, or perhaps looked at ego strength or object relations as discussed above? It is impossible to know of course, but if narratives are to be co-constructed and if we are always working at the margins of intersubjectivity it seems likely that as well as being a feeling/fact-gathering mission this initial meeting was also a struggle between strangers to find common ground. To resist the invitation or amplify difference so early on is likely to preclude the possibility of a therapeutic relationship developing at all. Nevertheless, the rush to a positive working alliance could also defend against the client's envy of the therapist's imagined children and the risks reinforcing the repression. Maybe therapists are as open to being seduced as being seductive, and the private practitioner arguably is more vulnerable to this kind of dynamic because of the need to earn a living, no matter how much an appropriately neutral therapeutic attitude is consciously cultivated.

Conclusion

If therapists insist that the assessment interview is a wholly objective process, there are two major pits into which they are likely to fall. One is to close down too early all the multiple possibilities in the client's narrative for the sake of therapeutic consistency and the other is to deny their own involvement and need. Both potentially lead to a sterile and collusive experience where nothing new arrives and nothing can be challenged.

Additionally in assessment it is not the lack of objective conclusions which have value but its provisional quality. What remains are narrative considerations at once both determined by the intersubjective relating of client and therapist and caught within a matrix where maybe there is little certainty, and where a different dyad might well come up with a different set of ideas. What is toxic for one therapist may not be so for another. Through the intellectual, emotional and countertransferential considerations of the material gleaned during the initial interview, the therapist becomes part of the client's story and a structure for the subsequent work emerges. As private practice does not need to account for its activities through notions such as NHS care plans, for example, that this may or may not turn out to be fictitious becomes less relevant.

Where assessment has benefit then is in providing a space for a joint story, and to some extent this is achieved through its distancing effect. By triangulating the therapeutic dyad, it provides a theoretical space for contemplation. As Searles (1965) has memorably pointed out, it is distance that permits thinking by removing the therapist one step away from the catastrophic anxiety of the client's resistance and ambivalence which, as can be seen above, is both disturbing and potentially contaminating. So although there are no guarantees and none should be offered in ethical practice (although it is always tempting to reassure), a kind of working title emerges. That this may conflict with the ideas of other organizations or other branches of therapy gives diversity and pluralism which in our postmodern and fragmented world can be the only option. Life is not a Chinese puzzle.

Notes

1 The terms 'psychotherapy' and 'counselling' will be referred to as 'therapy' from now on.
2 Mearns (1998) maintains that optimal numbers of clients who can be seen at any one time is dependent on ten variables related to clinical complexity, therapist experience and available support. The first assessment session is a crucial place to begin considering these.
3 Coltart (1993) sees assessments as a welcome diversion offering '*a different, colourful dimension to the everyday life of a therapist*' when one is restricted to a limited number of regular patients in full-time private practice.
4 White and Stancombe (2003) highlight the importance of not only listening to the patient but also listening to the self: moving from '*practising reflexively to practising reflexivity*' (p. 158).

References

Berkwitz, R. (1998) Assessment for psychoanalytic psychotherapy: an overview of the literature, in J. Cooper and H. Alfille (eds) *Assessment in Psychotherapy*, London: Karnac.

Birtle, J. and Buckingham, C. (1995) Building a cognitive model of psychotherapy assessment, in C. Mace (ed.) *The Art and Science of Assessment*, London: Routledge.

Coltart, N. (1993) *How to Survive as a Psychotherapist*, London: Sheldon Press.

CORE System Group (1998) *Clinical Outcomes in Routine Evaluation (CORE)*, Leeds: Psychological Therapies Research Centre, University of Leeds.

Davis, A. (1998) The significance of the opening story, in J. Cooper and H. Alfille (eds) *Assessment in Psychotherapy*, London: Karnac.

Denman, C. (1995) What is the point of a formulation?, in C. Mace (ed.) *The Art and Science of Assessment*, London: Routledge.

Elliot, A. (1994) *Psychoanalytic Theory – An Introduction*, Oxford: Blackwell.

Etchegoyen, H. (1991) *The Fundamentals of Psychoanalytic Technique*, London: Karnac.

Fink, B. (1997) *A Clinical Introduction to Lacanian Psychoanalysis: Theory and Technique*, London: Harvard.

Freud, S. (1915) Observations of transference love, *Standard Edition*, Vol. 12, London: Hogarth Press.

Hinshelwood, R. (1995) Psychodynamic formulation in assessment, in C. Mace *The Art and Science of Assessment*, London: Routledge.

Holmes, J. (1995) Assessing for psychoanalytic psychotherapy, in C. Mace *The Art and Science of Assessment*, London: Routledge.

Klein, J. (1999) Assessment – what for? Who for?, *British Journal of Psychotherapy* 15(3): 333–345.

Lees, J. (1998) What is clinical counselling in context?, in J. Lees (ed.) *Clinical Counselling in Context*, London: Routledge.

Mace, C. (1995) *The Art and Science of Assessment*, London: Routledge.

Malan, D. (1979) *Individual Psychotherapy and the Science of Psychodynamics*, London: Butterworth.

Maynard, A. (2000) Economic issues, in N. Rowland and S. Goss *Evidence-Based Counselling and Psychological Therapies*, London: Routledge.

Mearns, D. (1998) *Counselling and Psychotherapy Workloads*, BACP information sheet G4: www.bacp.co.uk/members/info_sheets/G4 (updated 2004).

Milner, J. and O'Byrne, P. (2004) *Assessment in Counselling: Theory, Process and Decision Making*, London: Palgrave.

Ogden, T. (1989) The initial analytic meeting, in T. Ogden *The Primitive Edge of Experience*, New York: Jason Aronson.

Parker, I., Georquea, E., Harper, D., McLaughlin, T. and Stowell-Smith, M. (1995) *Deconstructing Psychopathology*, London: Sage.

Roth, A. D. and Fonagy, P. (1996) *What Works for Whom: A Critical Review of Psychotherapy Research*, New York: Guilford Press.

Rowland, N. and Goss, S. (2000) *Evidence-Based Counselling and Psychological Therapies*, London: Routledge.

Rycroft, C. (1995) On beginning treatment, *British Journal of Psychotherapy* 11(4): 514–521.

Searles, H. F. (1965) Problems of psychoanalytic supervision, in H. F. Searles *Collected Papers on Schizophrenia and Related Subjects*, London: Maresfield Library.

Syme, G. (1994) *Counselling in Independent Practice*, Maidenhead: Open University Press.

Tantam, D. (1995) Why assess?, in C. Mace *The Art and Science of Assessment*, London: Routledge.

Teitlebaum, S. (1990) Supertransference: the role of the supervisor's blind spots, *Psychoanalytic Psychology* 7(2): 243–258.

Tyndale, A. (1998) The difference between diagnosis and assessment in psychoanalytic psychotherapy, in J. Cooper and H. Alfille (eds) *Assessment in Psychotherapy*, London: Karnac.

White, S. and Stancombe, J. (2003) *Clinical Judgement in the Health and Welfare Professions*, Maidenhead: Open University Press.

Zindel, V. (1995) How we assess for short term cognitive behavioural therapy, in C. Mace (ed.) *The Art and Science of Assessment*, London: Routledge.

r professionals – support
rusion?

Adrian Hemmings

Introduction

Working as an independent counsellor or psychotherapist outside an organization can be experienced as an isolating endeavour. There is little communication with other professionals apart from regular contact with a clinical supervisor. However, on closer reflection, while we do not have direct contact with other professionals, they can be present in a very indirect way. This may be experienced as supportive or it can lead to conflict that is played out in the therapeutic work. It is not just fellow professionals who constitute the 'other'; family, friends and even substances can impinge on the therapeutic relationship. In this chapter I examine some supportive elements of having the 'other' present in the background and then I go on to examine the potential conflict.

First I discuss medical back-up. When is it needed and if it is, what might the implications be to the counselling? Having another professional involved in the work with the client, even if this is in the background, can introduce the potential for splitting. I discuss the notion of splitting and some of the dilemmas that this process might create. Such issues as the effects of medication, psychiatric back-up and the difficulties that could arise when involving 'another' are discussed. Clients referred from medical practitioners (and indeed complementary therapists (see Robert Withers' Chapter 7)) may have expectations of counselling and of shared care which need to be clarified from the start of the work. The implications of this in independent practice are discussed. I then go on to talk about other forms of support such as clinical supervision, peer networks and continuing professional development (CPD) as a way of keeping in touch with the latest advances in the field. This in itself can be a support. How this could be developed in independent practice is discussed and its implications are examined. Similarly, recent research, often far from the mind of an independent practitioner, is also explored.

As part of most practitioners' initial contract, the limits of confidentiality are spelled out and these should include potential harm to self and others (in particular children). If these limits are exceeded what happens next and when should professionals such as social workers be contacted?

A completed suicide by a client may involve a number of other professionals, some of whom may be experienced as far from supportive. This can be a devastating event for a counsellor both on a personal and professional level. Managing the anxiety when a client has suicidal ideation and deciding when confidentiality is no longer therapeutic are tasks that take on an added dimension when working in independent practice.

Next I examine the influence of a 'significant other'. While present in all settings, when the therapist is working as an individual, there is more potential for the boundaries to become more blurred between him or her and the client's significant other and so for the therapist to experience more intrusion.

Finally, there are occasions when other professionals who have specific expertise need to be contacted. Using substance misuse as an example, I address issues such as how this should be done (if at all) and examine the implications. The substance itself may represent another and the way in which this can be managed is also reviewed.

Medical back-up

The relationship between psychotherapy and medicine (and hence counselling) is a long one (Tallis 1998). It is perhaps because of this that it is routine practice for many therapists to include contact details of the client's GP as part of the initial information gathering. How and why this information is collected may not have been fully thought through. Some counsellors contact their client's GP as a matter of course before the therapy begins, while others only use it in a medical emergency or on rare occasions when current medication needs to be discussed. Direct contact with the client's GP is an exceptional occurrence. The knowledge that if there is a severe deterioration with the client (such as suicidal ideation or a descent into psychosis) the fact that medical support is available in the background can be very reassuring for the counsellor, particularly if starting work with a client about whom she or he has concerns. This support can take the form of a future referral to psychiatric services or simple information on what local services are available. It can also take the form of a procedural action in case of future investigation or legal action. The boundaries around potential future contact and client's expectations of collaborative care (Seaburn *et al.* 1996) between the counsellor and the GP need to be clearly spelled out with the GP at the beginning. Unclear boundaries can create future conflict. So far I have described direct contact with a GP either by phone or by letter, however it is usually the indirect contact that is the most influential and it is this that can sow the seeds for splitting.

Splitting

The notion of splitting is based in psychodynamic theory and was originally developed by Anna Freud (Ekins and Freeman 1998). It is a projective process that enables the individual to manage positive and negative emotions by projecting them on to others. In some cases the counsellor may be the 'good' object and the GP the 'bad' object. This is something that can be very seductive to the counsellor at first, but if splitting occurs it is likely that when the client starts to have negative feelings about the counsellor (i.e. the counsellor starts to become human) they may well switch their projections. At this point the counsellor finds him or herself occupying the negative side of the split and as such may well be 'punished' for not being as 'ideal' as was assumed in the first instance. This is something that can be reflected upon when the counsellor notices that the client is idealizing one person but demonizing another. The potential for the client to split between the counsellor and his or her GP is increased when the client has been referred by the GP. In this instance, the client who may previously have had a caring relationship with their GP may have already experienced the referral out to the counsellor as a rejection or a statement that they are 'uncontainable'.

The different models used by health professions to understand their patients can also exacerbate this splitting. For example, the use of diagnosis is an essential part of a doctor's way of working and is not necessarily so readily used by a counsellor who is likely to be more focused on process (Weiner and Shere 1998). Thus a patient who presents with a diagnosis of 'clinical depression' may have difficulty in grasping the concept of trying to understand how they 'depress' themselves. After all, if a client has an illness then they are its victim and have little or no responsibility for it. This may be very freeing to the client, particularly if they are apt to blame themselves, but it also means that they therefore have little agency to change.

The GP and the counsellor are often in a position of power in relation to the client (Guggenbühl-Craig 1982). This too can exacerbate the potential for splitting as both professionals unconsciously vie for the position of 'lead carer'. A counsellor in independent practice may feel particularly vulnerable if working in isolation and therefore not having institutional status.

Identity is also an important aspect of diagnosis. 'I am a depressive or an alcoholic' are powerful beliefs that, if challenged, can lead to confrontation. A counsellor presented with a client who is wedded to a diagnosis is faced with yet another dilemma. If the counsellor confronts the belief of illness then the retort could be 'but my doctor says I have depression', thereby inviting the counsellor to split. If this is not addressed it could leave the client feeling confused and alienated; caught between two professionals that may well resonate with his or her earlier experience. An example of this, and perhaps one of the main differences in the use of model between medical doctors and counsellors, is in relation to medication.

Medication

Antidepressant medication is commonly prescribed and often used in isolation of psychological therapy (NICE 2004). If a client is improving and, in the counsellor's view, not in obvious need of medication, how can this be managed with the client? There are a number of issues that may be present in working with a patient who is on medication. The very fact that they are on medication means that they are in the 'care' of another, which will mean that they have had at least one consultation when they discussed their difficulties. It is likely that these difficulties will have been viewed within a different paradigm (i.e. more biomedical) and it may well be the task of the therapist to introduce the psychosocial balance without being embroiled in a Cartesian debate of 'either mind or body'. The patient will not only have a relationship with their other 'carer' but also with their medication. This may be a positive experience in the form of their 'reliable friend'. Here their medication takes on the role of a reliable other 'who' will always be there for them and 'who' is predictable and non-judgemental. Alternatively, they may feel more ambivalent about their use of medication and believe that they have to comply with their doctor by taking it.

Let me give an example. I had been working with a client for just under a year. She had presented with symptoms of depression that had gradually improved over time as she became more aware in the therapy of the cyclical pattern of her distress. She had also become aware of how she had developed ways of thinking and being from early childhood experiences that had contributed to these cycles and how this was sometimes played out in the therapy room. Towards the end of the year her partner died suddenly. She was very distressed and felt that her 'depression' was returning. She had suicidal ideation and became very frightened by this. Unknown to me she went to her GP who immediately prescribed amytryptyline. This is an older type of antidepressant that is inexpensive but does have some unpleasant side effects and is very toxic when taken as an overdose. She told me that she had not mentioned her suicidal thoughts to the GP who had, I presumed, prescribed the amytryptyline as a cost-cutting exercise.

This left me with a number of dilemmas. Why had she gone to the GP without discussing this with me and how was I to communicate my concern to her without getting into 'I know better than the GP', thereby inviting a split? We were able to discuss these issues and she was able to clarify her concerns about whether depression was a medical illness and as such should be treated by a medical doctor. She was also able to return to her GP and describe her suicidal thoughts. This resulted in a rapid change of prescription to a less toxic but more expensive seratonin specific reuptake inhibitor (SSRI). Ironically, and possibly because of this intervention, she no longer felt suicidal and did not feel she needed medication. She was now able to explore her medication seeking in terms of punishing me for not being as 'effective' as she had hoped. She continued to grieve and became less and less depressed.

Dependence

The above case vignette is an example of someone who did not develop a dependency on her medication. However, issues of physical or psychological dependence on the medication may arise that add another dynamic to the work. The client's reliance on an 'other' and how this is managed may have important implications for the therapeutic relationship. Again, there is an obvious opportunity for splitting here, not only by the client but also by the counsellor and the GP, the latter two possibly seeing themselves as rivals (Weiner and Shere 1998).

The intrusion of the other can take place when a client does become psychologically or physiologically dependent on medication. Again the counsellor is left with the dilemma of how to address the issue in isolation of the person who is prescribing the medication. If, in the counsellor's view, the client is dependent on their medication, he or she may be left 'holding the secret' and bound by the confidentiality agreement not to address the problem with the prescriber without the client's consent. Clearly this is something that would need to be addressed by the counsellor with the client.

Adherence

Another issue that can create a dilemma is that of adherence. There is a danger that patients who have been prescribed antidepressants take subtherapeutic doses that leave them with some of the side effects of the medication but without the therapeutic effects (Vergouwen *et al.* 2003). This happens for a variety of reasons, not least because patients believe that by taking less medication they will do themselves less harm. Should this be made evident to the counsellor (that their client is not adhering to the prescribed dose), once again it leaves the counsellor holding a secret between the client and their doctor. Clearly this requires the counsellor to have a basic knowledge of psychopharmacology, but if he or she does, then reflecting on this is important, as is a suggestion to the client that they discuss it with their GP. However, this does potentially intrude on the therapeutic relationship and once again fantasies about the counsellor's attitudes to medication and their relationship with the medical doctor may abound.

Primary and side effects of medication

An obvious difficulty that is encountered by counsellors working with clients on medication is the need to distinguish between the effects caused by the medication and those caused by what is said or thought in the room. There is clear conflict here between two paradigms: the biomedical paradigm, which is largely aimed at alleviating the 'symptoms'; and notions of 'experiencing and working through' which are likely to be part of the counsellor's philosophy. The primary effects of medication are too numerous to examine in this chapter (see the *British National Formulary*, Mehta 2006), but those medications that induce a sedating effect are particularly pertinent to counselling. The main medication in this category is the benzodiazapine (benzos) group and in some cases beta blockers. Benzos are used to suppress affect which, if a client is consistently overanxious, is useful in the short term. However, the downside of benzos is that they can also create dependence and interfere with cognitive abilities. It may be that a certain amount of anxiety is desirable to facilitate change.

Not knowing if a 'relaxed client' is simply an effect of their medication, a result of an overall psychological improvement or simply that they are 'cut off' from their emotional world can prove frustrating and deskilling for the counsellor. Once again the 'other' has intruded into the relationship and how this is managed is important for both client and counsellor. Again, a basic knowledge of psychopharmacology is an important first step, and some understanding of the dosage that the client is being prescribed is also important. However, the dilemma for the counsellor is how this frustration is managed. Knowing that the medication has been prescribed by another professional who is likely to be operating from within a different paradigm can prove difficult. Once again the counsellor is faced with the dilemma of how this can be addressed without being involved in a split and possible competition with the prescriber.

Similar issues arise when considering side effects. The side effects, principally with the older antidepressants, are numerous (Mehta 2006). Again the counsellor is left wondering if what they observe is an aspect of the counselling or of medication. Some of these side effects can be particularly unpleasant and the counsellor may well be drawn into the adherence debate.

When I have been faced with this problem I have reflected to the client their lack of affect when describing what was to me an extremely distressing event. I have wondered with them whether this response was something that had always been with them or whether it had occurred since they had been taking the medication. If it proved likely that this was a result of taking the medication, we have been able to discuss the merits and disadvantages of this so that the client is able to make the choice of where they go from here. This may or may not involve the client making an appointment with their GP to discuss their medication levels. I have had to work with the consequences of both decisions. The very act of noticing this may invite the client to have fantasies about my attitudes to medication which need to be explored as part of the decision-making process. This enables the client to own their decision as much as possible. However, there is still the risk that in order to address the issue with the GP the client will frame the consultation in terms of a directive from the therapist. The fact that this still leaves the door open for splitting is a dilemma that I have to manage. This example describes how counsellor and client attitudes towards medication need to be explored sensitively.

Counsellor and client attitudes to medication

As described above, the therapist may have his or her own attitudes to medication that may well be played out in communication with the GP via the client. There is also a considerable literature on client attitudes to medication and this was a major focus on the 'defeat depression campaign' (Paykel *et al.* 1998). It was found that the majority of participants held negative views on antidepressants and would prefer a form of 'talking therapy'. The fact that a client has come to a private counsellor in the first place probably suggests that they prefer counselling to medication. Counsellors may also tend to harbour negative views on medication, sometimes viewing it as a direct challenge to their work. If both client and counsellor hold these negative views then it is likely that they are played out overtly if the counsellor advises the client to stop medication, or covertly by the non-verbal communication between counsellor and client. Either way the potential for splitting is obvious.

Collegial support

Supervision

Just as counsellors work in different ways so do supervisors, and it is important that there is a workable match (Bramely 1996;

McMahon *et al.* 2005). Clearly if the supervisor uses a purely psychodynamic model and the counsellor works using an integrative model, what could be a supportive experience may end in conflict and the counsellor feeling deskilled. It is important that through an experience of 'good enough' (Winnicott 1971) supervision the counsellor develops a sense of an 'internal supervisor' (Casement 1985) or 'self supervisor' (Bramely 1996) who is critical yet supportive and not one that is merely persecutory. This may be particularly pertinent when a counsellor is relatively inexperienced and has yet to develop their individual style.

Latest developments and research

An often-neglected source of support is that of research. Many practitioners have an ambivalent attitude towards research; after all, how can you measure the immeasurable? However, much of the research in psychotherapy and counselling has moved on from the question of whether counselling works. The focus is now an enquiry into how it works, with which clients (Hemmings 1999) and more recently by which counsellors (Norcross 2002). In other words, research is becoming more practitioner friendly and we are moving away from evidence-based practice to practice-based evidence. Research into what goes on in the room and the type and timing of interventions offers much more relevance to practitioners and can be experienced as a form of support.

Most counselling journals have a research column and some journals are devoted to psychotherapy research (e.g. *Psychotherapy Research* published by the Society for Psychotherapy Research, or BACP's *Counselling and Psychotherapy Research*). Websites can also be a source of keeping up with the latest developments although some caution needs to be exercised as some have a clear agenda. Sites such as *talkingcure.com* and *allaboutpsychotherapy.com* are full of information about the latest research and ethical issues. *Talkingcure* also has an interesting and controversial section called 'Baloney watch' that examines the evidence for the latest claims for 'new improved wonder' therapies.

I have examined the most likely professionals who are likely to be present in the therapeutic relationship but other professionals may become relevant in specific situations.

Child protection

Working with clients who are currently under social services care is probably a rare occurrence in private practice, but may occur if the counsellor has a particular speciality such as substance misuse counselling. The dilemma in this instance is that of confidentiality. For instance, if a client has a child who is on the Child Protection Register then, according to the Children Act 2004, information about the client's progress must be made available to social services on request. This means that in theory the counsellor could be contacted and asked to give a progress report on a client which could make the difference between the client's children remaining with them or being taken into care. Clearly this will have an effect on the therapeutic relationship where the counsellor is in a position of legal as well a therapeutic power. Because of this, it is important that the ground rules of the relationship are spelled out at the beginning of the therapy so that the counsellor is not left in the insidious position of suddenly having to tell the client that they will be giving vital information about the counselling sessions to a third party. Even if the ground rules are clearly defined, the nature of the counselling is different in these circumstances and the counsellor's customary neutral stance cannot be possible in the eyes of the client.

The concept of confidentiality in different professions is often interpreted in very different ways and the notion of (almost) complete confidentiality between counsellor and client may be anathema to a medical doctor or social worker (Seaburn *et al.* 1966). This would set the scene for a potentially bruising encounter where statutory rights are used as a threat. Once again, if a counsellor is working in independent practice his or her lack of statutory power may exacerbate this.

Suicide

The effect of a client who completes suicide can be devastating to a counsellor even when working within a team (see Rosalind Field's Chapter 10). However, when working in independent practice this can be particularly difficult. With no colleagues to reflect upon your work with the client and to discuss the 'if only' questions, loneliness and isolation may be a difficulty. This needs to be addressed. The importance of effective and supportive supervision is particularly relevant and having the space to reflect on the counselling practice prior to a potential suicide needs to take place. The periods immediately before and immediately after a client suicide are crucial.

If the counsellor realizes that a client is intent on suicide, who if anyone should they contact? After a suicide it is likely that an autopsy enquiry will be held to which the counsellor may be summoned. This becomes more likely if a psychological autopsy (Hawton *et al.* 1998, 2004) is conducted which examines the client's interactions with the counsellor prior to the completion of suicide. As there is unlikely to be a formal avenue of support to those working in independent practice, this process can be experienced as supportive or punitive depending on how it is conducted. Counsellors may be called as witness to an enquiry and may be asked to submit session notes and action records, and are advised to record their actions taken before the suicide. Once more the other impinges on the relationship. However, recording actions taken and being extra vigilant over session notes is a communication to someone other than the counsellor or the client and is likely to have an effect on the work in the room. For instance, interventions that may have an element of risk such as challenging statements or interpretations, or paradoxical interventions such as those that are sometimes adopted with parasuicidal clients may be kept to a minimum because of possible legal consequences (Cummings and Sayama 1995).

The ethical dilemmas facing the counsellor between the clients right to 'self administered euthanasia' or suicide being an expression of 'mental illness' are elegantly discussed by Bond (2000). Linked to this anxiety-driven practice is the evidence that when working with clients who display suicidal ideation counsellors are reticent about addressing this with the client and making a risk assessment (Reeves *et al.* 2004).

If a client has made clear plans to kill themselves the necessity to break confidentiality is contentious and poses another dilemma for the counsellor (Bond 2000). Issues such as clinical responsibility, medical back-up and defensive practice (back covering) all play a part in this. BACP guidelines on this (written in 2002) are rather vague:

> Situations in which clients pose a risk of causing serious harm to themselves or others are particularly challenging for the

practitioner. These are situations in which the practitioner should be alert to the possibility of conflicting responsibilities between those concerning their client, other people who may be significantly affected, and society generally. Resolving conflicting responsibilities may require due consideration of the context in which the service is being provided. Consultation with a supervisor or experienced practitioner is strongly recommended, whenever this would not cause undue delay. In all cases, the aim should be to ensure for the client a good quality of care that is as respectful of the client's capacity for self-determination and their trust as circumstances permit . . . Any disclosures should be undertaken in ways that best protect the client's trust. Practitioners should be willing to be accountable to their clients and to their profession for their management of confidentiality in general and particularly for any disclosures made without their client's consent.

Even if sensitively done (i.e. giving the client the opportunity to inform others before the counsellor does), breaking confidentiality will affect the relationship and it is likely that the client will be more self-censoring if they know that what they are about to say is probably going to be disclosed to a third party. It may be that the therapist's containment of the relationship allows the client to work their way out of their suicidal thoughts. On the other hand, the anxiety that this creates, particularly in a counsellor working in isolation in independent practice, may be intolerable (and unjustified) to the counsellor. In this case who is the disclosure for?

Breaching confidentiality

Confidentiality in other areas of the client's life poses more dilemmas for the counsellor in private practice. There are legal requirements for the counsellor to break confidentiality in certain circumstances and these are discussed in detail by Jenkins (1997; also see Hudson-Allez in Chapter 2). For example, there are circumstances when where two laws are in conflict with each other one will override due to a hierarchy of laws. For instance, laws that enforce confidentiality are currently the Human Rights Act 2000 and the Data Protection Act 1998 and those that override these are section 18 of the prevention of Terrorism Act, section 9 and schedule 1 of the Police and Criminal Evidence Act 1984 and section 52 of the Drug Trafficking Act 1994. Once again, the 'other' intrudes.

Significant others

While a client's significant other is usually indirectly present in most counselling situations, they can be especially influential in private practice, particularly when the counsellor is working from home. It is perhaps the potential intimacy of visiting another's home that can engender a number of fantasies; something that working from a clinic or within a team does not create to such an extent (see Rosalind Field's Chapter 8 on working from home). It can be difficult for one partner when the other is seen to be receiving 'unlimited support and affection' and 'being advised' to change aspects of the relationship which may have been the very things that have kept the relationship together for several years. Having one person changing in a relationship while the other is not or does not wish to can be daunting and anxiety provoking. This can take the form of quizzing the client on their return from therapy or open hostility towards the therapist who is envied for their special intimate relationship with the client. The client may also have an investment in discussing their therapy with a partner and actively enjoy playing them off against the therapist, particularly if the partner and the therapist are of the same sex. The possible Oedipal origins of this are obvious (Klein 1928). However, the attempts of the 'significant other' to 'mess up' (Klein 1957) the intimate relationship between therapist and client and have more involvement themselves can vary from simple criticism of the therapist to, in extreme cases, direct attempts to intimidate.

For example, I had a client who described her husband's concerns about her counselling sessions. My client described how he would be waiting at the door on her return and ask for a detailed description of the sessions. We discussed what this might mean to her and how she was being positioned (and positioned herself) in the relationship as the 'presenting patient'. We reflected on this and she developed ways of addressing it with her husband. Once she felt that she had resolved this, her husband started to phone me with messages telling me that she would be late or cancelling a session; he was acting as her secretary. During these calls he would sometimes invite me to comment on progress and time scales. Obviously I did not comment, but reflecting on these calls with my client enabled her to throw more light on her role in the relationship. This eventually led them both to seek couple counselling.

The involvement of a significant other is not necessarily a negative occurrence and may depend on the model being used by the counsellor. Some therapists think that the therapeutic space is almost sacrosanct and invite the client to adopt a 'no leakage rule' whereby what happens in the therapy room stays there. Others actively engage the significant other, for example, when a client is asked to map out a case conceptualization (Greenberger and Padesky 1995). Here the client creates a diagram of a cyclical path of behaviours, feelings and cognitions that end up in a familiar and usually negative position. In this instance the involvement of a partner or family member can be extremely valuable, particularly when identifying behaviours.

Splitting, as discussed in the section on medical back-up, can also be present when a significant other is involved. This can be on the part of the therapist who might view the client as the victim in a relationship and may be seduced into attempting to rescue the client and criticize their partner. As mentioned above, the therapist may be viewed as a rival by the partner and the jealousy of the imagined intimacy between the therapist and their partner may be unbearable.

Working with substance misuse

I have chosen to include a separate section on substance misuse as it can illustrate two issues: first, the dilemma the counsellor may have if they feel deskilled in working specifically with clients with substance use difficulties; second, the relationship that the client has with their substance of choice. Most counsellors in independent practice will encounter clients who have difficulties with substance use and they do often feel deskilled. This is probably due to the fact that most counselling trainings do not include substance misuse counselling in their syllabus. The issues arising from the use of substances by a client have been largely covered above in the discussion on medication. Like medication, the effects, after effects and side effects of substances can equally cloud the consciousness of a client. The relationship that the client has with their substance of choice can also affect the way in which they relate to the counsellor. However, apart from a dealer the presence of 'the other' is not as evident as with medication. Here a dilemma that faces some counsellors is whether they should suggest that the client address their substance misuse with a substance misuse specialist. Many counsellors feel that a specialist should 'deal' with that aspect of the client. There is strength in this argument. It is probably unlikely that the client is going to make best use of the counselling if they continue to misuse substances.

Helping a client to address their substance misuse behaviour and gain control of it is an important first step before a more reflective stance can be adopted. However, one of the difficulties of referring to a specialist is the notion that substance misuse is a different and therefore separate aspect of the client that needs to be split off and dealt with elsewhere. Someone who is misusing substances is likely to be fragmented in the first place and there is a danger that referral elsewhere may exacerbate this fragmentation. Does the counsellor attempt to help the client to address their misuse without the necessary skills and training and risk entering into an impasse, or should they refer out and risk a split in the client? If they do refer out, how could this potential split be minimized? A break in the counselling while the client works on their substance misuse may be a good enough compromise. Post-qualification training in working with this client group is probably a better option.

While not being specific to working in independent practice, another aspect of the impingement of the 'other' is the relationship that a client may have with their substance of choice. In this case the 'other' is the substance the client is using which in many clients may be anthropomorphized in a similar way that clients may relate to medication as described above. The substance may be a reliable friend who is always there for them and who never challenges them. It may be a nagging partner who is always on their back and making demands. There is therefore a likelihood that the way in which the substance is related to will impinge on the relationship between counsellor and client. For instance, if the substance is 'an old friend' and you as a counsellor may be challenging it, it is possible that they may resort to 'someone' who is more understanding, i.e. their substance.

I used to work with a client who had problems with his drinking. Using the 'cycle of change' model (Prochaska and DiClemente 1982) we established when and how he might relapse and considered ways of making this less likely. More physical exercise was one way and he agreed that he would join a rambling club and increase his social contacts as well as his physical stamina. After two weeks of not making any movement towards his goal, we explored how he had managed not to complete it. I wondered about his motivation and he determined to renew his attempts. The next week he almost triumphantly told me he had had a weekend of binging and that this was better than 'being hassled by me'. At least he knew what to expect. When we reflected on this and how he had positioned me as the 'nagger' and the alcohol as the 'ally', we were able to explore this relationship in more detail. He began to recognize that in some ways he was drinking *at* me as a way of expressing how angry he was about me 'nagging' him. He started to recognize how familiar this was and how he tended to relate to others in terms of naggers or friends, that is, in terms of his core conflictual relationship (Book 1998); 'you are either with me or against me', a pattern that was particularly relevant to his relationship with his partner. In understanding this way of relating we were able to explore more useful forms of relationship.

Conclusion

In this chapter I have discussed how one of the most positive aspects of working as part of an organization is the potential support that it offers. As a therapist working in this context you are not alone in your work and in an ideal organization, if things get difficult, there are colleagues to consult, staff meetings to attend, procedures to follow, administrative back-up and a framework in which to contact other professionals. Even if the organization is not the ideal one pictured above, and it is likely that underlying dynamics examined in Chapter 6 on group practice will be present, there is usually some support or contact available. This contact with other colleagues and professionals, be it direct or indirect, is done within a recognized system and hopefully communication lines are predetermined. However, few if any of these support networks exist when working as an independent practitioner, even more so when working from home. It is up to the practitioner to ensure that they create support systems and ways of communicating with other professionals, some of whom may have differing models of practice and understanding of the 'problem'.

As has been discussed in this chapter, it is the indirect intrusion of the 'other' that needs to be kept in mind when working with clients who may also be involved in another health care system.

The way in which an independent practitioner manages these two systems can result in a hindrance to the work. However, when skilfully managed they can offer an additional level to the therapeutic relationship which can prove invaluable in times of crisis.

References

Bond, T. (2000) *Standards and Ethics for Counselling in Action*, London: Sage.

Book, H. E. (1998) *How to Practice Brief Psychodynamic Psychotherapy. The Core Conflictual Relationship Theme Method*, Washington, DC: APA.

Bramely, W. (1996) *The Supervisory Couple in Broad-Spectrum Psychotherapy*, London: Free Association Books.

Casement, P. (1985) *On Learning from the Patient*, London: Tavistock.

Children Act 2004, London: The Stationery Office.

Cummings, N. and Sayama, M. (1995) *Focused Psychotherapy. A Casebook of Brief Intermittent Psychotherapy Throughout the Life Cycle*, New York: Brunner/Mazel.

Ekins, R. and Freeman, R. (1998) *Anna Freud: Selected Writings*, Harmondsworth: Penguin.

Greenberger, D. and Padesky, C. (1995) *Mind Over Mood*, New York: Guilford Press.

Guggenbühl-Craig, A. (1982) *Power in the Helping Relationships*, Dallas: Spring Publications.

Hawton, K., Appleby, L., Platt, S., Foster, T., Cooper, J., Malmber, A. *et al.* (1998) The psychological autopsy approach to studying suicide: a review of methodological issues, *Journal of Affective Disorders* 50: 269–276.

Hawton, K., Malmberg, A. and Simkin, S. (2004) Suicide in doctors: a psychological autopsy study, *Journal of Psychosomatic Research* 57: 1–4.

Hemmings, A. (1999) Assessment of psychological change and the future practice of clinical counselling, in J. Lees (ed.) *Clinical Counselling in Context*, London: Routledge.

Jenkins, P. (1997) *Counselling Psychotherapy and the Law*, London: Sage.

Klein, M. (1928) Early stages of the oedipus conflict, *International Journal of Psychoanalysis* 9: 167–180.

—— (1957) *Envy and Gratitude: A Study of Unconscious Forces*, New York: Basic Books.

McMahon, G., Palmer, S. and Wilding, C. (2005) *The Essential Skills for Setting Up a Counselling and Psychotherapy Practice*, London: Routledge.

Mehta, D. (ed.) (2006) *British National Formulary (BNF)*, London: BMJ and RPS Publishing.

National Institute for Clinical Excellence Guidelines (NICE, 2004) *NICE Guidelines to Improve the Treatment and Care of People with Depression and Anxiety*, London: NICE.

Norcross, D. (2002) Empirically supported therapy relationships, in J. C. Norcross (ed.) *Psychotherapy Relationships that Work. Therapist Contributions and Responsiveness to Patients*, Oxford: Oxford University Press.

Paykel, E. S., Hart, D. and Priest, R. G. (1998) Changes in public attitudes to depression during the Defeat Depression Campaign, *British Journal of Psychiatry* 173: 519–522.

Prochaska, J. O. and DiClemente, C. C. (1982) Transtheoretical therapy: toward a more integrative model of change, *Psychotherapy: Theory, Research and Practice* 19: 276–288.

Reeves, A., Bowl, R., Wheeler, S. and Guthrie, E. (2004) The hardest words: exploring the dialogue of suicide in the counselling process – a discourse analysis, *Counselling and Psychotherapy Research* 4(1): 62–71.

Seaburn, D., Lorenz, A., Gunn, W., Gawinski, B. and Mauksch, L. (1996) *Models of Collaboration. A Guide for Mental Health Professionals Working with Health Care Practitioners*, New York: Basic Books.

Tallis, F. (1998) *Changing Minds: The History of Psychotherapy as an Answer to Human Suffering*, London: Cassell.

Vergouwen, A., Bakker, A., Katon, W., Verheij, T. and Koerselman, F. (2003) Improving adherence to antidepressants: a systematic review of interventions, *Journal of Clinical Psychiatry* 64(12): 1415–1420.

Weiner, J. and Shere, M. (1998) *Counselling and Psychotherapy in Primary Health Care: A Psychodynamic Approach*, London: Macmillan Press.

Winnicott, D. W. (1971) *Playing and Reality*, London: Tavistock.

Chapter 6

The individual therapist working in an independent group practice
Unconscious dynamics and defensive practices
Andrea Halewood and Jeremy Christey

Introduction

As an alternative to the relative isolation of working from home or from rented consulting rooms, the private counsellor or psycho-therapist may choose to work within a group practice. Group practices may vary from a group of therapists working in the same building though running their practices in isolation, to more structured organizations which may include therapists of widely differing theoretical orientations and experiences. The group may or may not have a practice manager or head, and may or may not consist of practitioners who work in the same way with the same client group. The group may share premises or may only share an answering machine. However, even the smallest, unstructured organization will have its own particular unconscious pressures and organizational defence systems to deal with.

In this chapter I will attempt to elucidate how the individual therapist working within the group practice can be affected by the unconscious dynamics of the group and by the primitive defensive practices which organizations may utilize to ward off anxiety. I have found from my own experience that failure to think about, address and work through these issues can lead to problems being acted out within groups of clinicians and group workers; the negative impact on all involved can then seriously undermine clinical practice.

It can be helpful to have a theoretical framework in mind to help us think about the culture in which we work and to this end I have found the ideas of psychoanalytic theorists such as Freud, Klein and Bion invaluable when considering both the conscious and the unconscious dynamics in operation within groups and organizations. In the first part of this chapter I will be outlining these ideas and attempting to illustrate them with a composite case example drawn from my own clinical practice. I wish to argue that the ability to think about these defences will help the individual practitioner to develop conscious strategies for dealing with them, while the capacity to acknowledge, work through and ultimately relinquish defensive strategies will facilitate the personal development of both the individual and the group.

What do we as individual practitioners bring to the group?

The choices we make regarding which profession to train for, that is, psychoanalyst, psychotherapist, psychologist, counsellor; which therapeutic model to use, which client group we choose to work with and in what kind of setting are all influenced by our own unresolved unconscious issues. Bion (1968) referred to this tendency as *valency*, which he described as 'the individual's readiness to enter into combination with the group in making and acting on the basic assumptions' (Bion 1968). Bion argued that this propensity towards an unconscious group dynamic gives rise to collective defences against the anxieties stirred up by the work in hand which can seriously impede the ability of the group to perform the assigned task.

A further complicating factor for therapists to consider is that those attracted to the helping professions often suffer from unresolved narcissistic issues and these will impact on the group. Racusin *et al.* (1981) studied the impact of therapists' early family experiences on career choice and found that three-quarters of therapists were involved in caretaking within the family in one form or another, either 'parenting' or 'counselling'. Glickauf-Hughes and Mehlman (1995) suggest that these individuals are therefore unlikely to have had their own narcissistic needs met, and will therefore have suffered narcissistic injury. Therapists with this background often struggle with issues such as perfectionism, audience sensitivity and unstable self-esteem. It has also been suggested that rage, anger and hostility are also central to the life of those with unresolved narcissistic issues (Raskin *et al.* 1991).

As Glickauf-Hughes and Mehlman (1995) point out, becoming a therapist involves periods of doubt and uncertainty. The work lacks structure and can therefore be frustrating for those who need a concrete sense of achievement (Hinshelwood 1985). In addition, as Mollon (1989) suggests, the nature of the transference and projection processes may cause the therapist to feel ineffective as he or she is constantly probed and provoked by his or her clients. Patients will often use defences and projections which therapists, particularly trainees, have a tendency to internalize. Consequently, therapists will frequently struggle with doubts and insecurities about being 'good enough' (Glickauf-Hughes and Mehlman 1995). These factors make therapists particularly vulnerable to getting caught up in the institutional defences arising from shared anxieties.

The group – apart from or a part of?

In addition to the unconscious issues the individual may bring to the group, group membership can be perceived to be a mixed blessing. While the group may offer certain benefits and be perceived as protective, it may also feel restrictive and inhibiting. As Bion suggests: 'the individual is impelled to seek the satisfaction of his needs in his group and is at the same time inhibited in this aim by the primitive fears that the group arouses' (Bion 1968).

Wolfenstein (1990), drawing on Bion's theories, argues that an understanding of group psychology can help us to know why it is that individuals both feel alienated and yet submerge themselves in groups. Freud suggested that primitive fears cause the individual within the group to regress to a more infantile condition, and this regression causes a loss of his 'individual distinctiveness' (Freud 1921: 9). This loss can lead to feelings of depersonalization and an attempt to separate from the group in the interests of regaining or protecting individuality. Bion suggests, however, that separation is never truly possible, that the individual is 'and always has been, a member of a group, even if his membership of it consists of behaving in such a way that reality is given to an idea that he does not belong to a group at all' (Bion 1968).

This struggle between being *apart from* and *a part of* the group is illuminated by a cursory glance at therapists' advertisements for their services in the local telephone directory. While independent practitioners are keen to emphasize their separate identity and brand image, even individual practitioners may still prefer to describe themselves as Jo Bloggs 'Associates'. Descriptions of practitioners as being part of a larger group of which they are at the head seem to illustrate the desire to be, and to be seen to be, both part of a clinical, professional group yet boundaried and separate at the same time. However, as Wolfenstein has argued, '"the individual" is an element in a group fantasy' (Wolfenstein 1990).

The family as group prototype

Freud argued that the family group was the prototype of all groups and, following Freud, Wolfenstein has suggested that the experience of the individual in the group is similar to the relationship between mother and child: 'the ontogenetic foundation of group psychology is the relatively undifferentiated union of mother and infant' (Wolfenstein 1990). Stokes (1994) extends this analogy further by suggesting that organizational conflict and competition are akin to sibling rivalry, as individuals compete for resources and power within the group. Furthermore, in the same way that a child wishes to become like his parent, so adults may wish to assimilate the characteristics of someone they admire. In a group they may therefore identify with the group leader or practice manager, and in wishing to be like them unconsciously introject them into their ego, or sense of self. Freud described this unconscious process of 'identification' as 'the earliest expression of an emotional tie with another person' (Freud 1921: 60). He suggested that in a group situation the group is united by each member's '*introjective identification*' with the leader. 'The primal father is the group ideal which governs the ego in the place of the ego ideal' (Freud 1921: 100). Consequently, the leader of the group is able to exercise his authority in the group because he represents the group's ego ideal.

In contrast Bion suggested that rather than an *introjective* identification with the leader, each group member splits off parts of his ego and *projects* these into the chosen leader. As such the leader is chosen not for his outstanding interpersonal strengths and leadership ability, but because he is 'an individual whose personality renders him peculiarly susceptible to the obliteration of individuality by the basic assumption group's leadership requirements' (Bion 1968: 177). Consequently, the leader has no more individuality or freedom of action than any other group member. Bion also questioned Freud's concept of the family as the prototype for the group, arguing that Freud's view did not go far enough. Bion suggested instead that only the healthy group resembles the family group, whereas 'the more disturbed the group, the less it is likely to be understood on the basis of family patterns' (Bion 1968).

Anxiety – the group as container and protector

For the individual practitioner working alone, dealing with client's projections, distress and emotional needs is difficult, demanding and likely to arouse a great deal of anxiety. Practising within a group is one way for therapists to protect themselves. An effective group can increase the capacity to digest and translate clients' defensive behaviours and can increase the opportunities to observe and think about defensive practices. In this way co-workers can be a sanitizing influence and by providing containment can offer some protection from overwhelming anxieties. The interpersonal connection and informal support found in group practices and the attention and empathy of a fellow practitioner can be connecting and protective. As Vaillant and Vaillant (1990) found in a longitudinal study of US graduates, a sense of connection is protective of longer term health, and I suggest that this enables us to function as individual therapists, in much the same way that supervision does.

Furthermore, the decompression the group offers allows longer forays into the often disturbing internal world of the client and may increase our tolerance of this experience. Working within a group can be both a balancing and enlivening experience as we move back and forth between client work and the protection of the group. The containment that an effective group can offer may also prevent repetitive acting out between therapists and clients, for the group is also a norm against which you can measure yourself. How are you within this group? How do you act and react when presented with the differing members of the group? Differences you observe in your own responses can provide a sanitizing measure by which you can monitor your own reactions to both your fellow workers and to your clients.

Some common defensive practices

Stokes (1994) suggests that one of the psychological benefits with which an institution provides us is 'something that we can really love or something that we can really hate'. One of the unconscious reasons why we join organizations is that they provide us with opportunities to locate difficult and hated aspects of ourselves in some 'other', by means of the defensive processes of splitting and projective identification. So important is this function that loss of it through unemployment or redundancy can lead to high levels of emotional distress and a subsequent decline in mental functioning (Stokes 1994). As such, groups and institutions provide an essential psychological function in that they allow us to project those parts of ourselves that we wish to remain unconscious into the organization or other individuals within it.

Klein theorized that our earliest relationships are marked by the defensive processes of *projective identification, splitting* and *denial* and suggested that when we are facing unbearable anxiety we will fall back on these primitive defences. If suitably aware of our countertransference responses we may use these feelings to understand our clients' internal worlds better. If not, we may act out these feelings, either with our clients or within the group. However, if the group gets caught up in something contagious, a state of mind can be passed rapidly from person to another until everyone is afflicted and no one can retain the capacity to face reality. As Hirschhorn has pointed out, 'one person's anxiety may trigger an anxiety chain, through which anxiety becomes general' (Hirschhorn 1985).

By being aware of how this contagion can spread, we are better able to tackle issues in a direct and appropriate way. This awareness is essential. As therapists we are constantly invaded by clients' projections. However, if we are working within a group we may get drawn into avoiding understanding or handling what is projected into us and deal with our unprocessed emotions by projecting that which feels most difficult into the group. As Halton has pointed out, in the helping professions 'there is a tendency to deny feelings of hatred or rejection towards clients. These feelings may be more easily dealt with by projecting them' (Halton 1994).

Bion: the basic assumption groups and the work group

Bion argued that in order to be effective the group must remain in contact with reality, that is, be able to distinguish what is going on inside the group from what is located outside the group. If this insight is lacking, the group members will fall back on projective techniques to rid themselves of unbearable feelings of anxiety. The group can only regain its effectiveness when the source of the anxiety is located within the group and therefore the underlying issues can be worked through.

Central to Bion's theory of group behaviour is the proposal that whenever a group gathers together to perform a task it will behave as if the group holds shared unconscious attitudes, or basic assumptions which will influence the activity of the group. Basic assumptions are unconscious expressions of group anxiety and are held to defend members against anxiety. In this way 'the adult resorts, in what may be a massive regression, to mechanisms described by Melanie Klein as typical of the earliest phases of mental life' (Bion 1968).

The group operating on basic assumptions cannot do any useful work because all energies are concentrated on maintaining the group phantasy. As reality is not tested, the group fails to recognize that the shared anxieties do not reside outside the group but within it. One way that this might be addressed is by the employment of an external facilitator who can enter the group objectively from the outside and enable the group to see the dynamics that are being played out within it.

Bion argued that there are three quite distinct basic assumptions that any group may adopt which will affect the behaviour and the productivity of the group. Although only one basic assumption will be adopted at any one time, groups can switch rapidly between the three states, or assume the same basic assumption for the duration of the group. What all the basic assumptions share, however, is a reliance on the primitive, regressed defence mechanisms of splitting and projective identification to defend against anxiety. It is this defence that causes any group operating under a basic assumption to fail in its assigned task for, as de Board has pointed out, in defending ourselves against anxiety we are also defending ourselves against reality (de Board 1978).

The basic assumption of dependency (baD)

The group utilizing the basic assumption of dependency will have regressed to a state of inadequacy and immaturity. They will be looking to a leader on whom they can depend 'for nourishment, material and spiritual, and protection' (Bion 1968). Given this relinquishing of autonomy, the group will then have a powerful need to idealize their leader and believe him to be all knowing and all powerful. It is this idealization that prevents any new learning or development occurring, both on an individual and group level, and therefore renders the group ineffective.

The basic assumption of fight/flight (baF)

This group believes its shared purpose is defensive: either to fight something or to flee from it. As such this basic assumption is based on paranoia. Given the paranoid thinking of the group members, the leader is expected to take decisive action against an enemy, either real or imaginary. If no enemy exists the group will need to invent one. In believing that all danger resides outside the group rather than within it, the group has lost contact with reality and therefore no progress can be made.

The basic assumption of pairing (baP)

This group is characterized by hope which can be expressed in a variety of ways, such as hope for a better future. The unconscious fantasy is that two group members will pair off and provide a new leader for an imagined utopian future. However, this hope can be sustained only as long as the situation remains unchanged. If a leader were to be created then the group's hopes would be disappointed, as no leader could satisfy such idealized expectations. Again this basic assumption has a defensive function. The group's fantasy about what may happen obscures the reality of what is happening, so the group cannot progress.

The work group

Unlike the basic assumption groups, the work group is aware of reality and can distinguish between what is operating outside the group and inside. In addition, it knows that it has to learn and develop in order to perform the task in hand. In contrast, the basic assumption group operates by defending itself from external reality and these defences will vary between groups. As Hinshelwood and Skogstad (2002) suggest, 'specific forms of health-care lead to specific anxieties which create specific defense mechanisms'.

Observation: Southways Counselling Service

The following example is a composite picture of group dynamics and difficulties drawn from a number of agencies in which I have worked. The patterns involved can be understood using Bion's descriptions of the basic assumptions states (Bion 1968).

Southways Counselling Service was located in the same building as a number of other counselling agencies, all of which were financed and run by a local charity. Twenty-five student counsellors, all at different stages of their training at different training institutions, were on voluntary placement at the agency. Consequently, the student therapists utilized a range of different counselling models. In addition, the nine counselling rooms were used by ten private therapists who, unlike the students, were paid for their work. However, these differences were not discussed and did not even appear to be acknowledged. The dominant culture at Southways was one of co-operation. The counsellors all seemed to be pulling in the same direction, working hard to protect the quality of the milieu and the standard of the work offered.

The dominant culture

Hinshelwood and Skogstad (2002) have noted that the most important aspect of the dominant culture, or atmosphere of an organization lies in the 'expression of the defensiveness of the group or organization. It is the palpability of a defence in operation'. The dominant culture of Southways was strikingly positive. It appeared to be that of a warm, professional and containing environment and was idealized by the counsellors who worked there. They believed Southways to be a model of good practice and superior in many ways to other agencies. Consequently, newcomers were soon coerced into accepting the beliefs which had developed over time. It was difficult for counsellors to view the service objectively as they seemed resistant to spoiling the good atmosphere.

What was being avoided

Given the shortage of room space available, the number of counsellors competing for resources, the widely differing therapeutic approaches utilized and the varying levels of experience amongst the counsellors, there was a surprising avoidance of conflict within the agency. This was partly due to the lack of a group forum or meeting place. Students tended to stay in their rooms to write up their notes following sessions, thereby avoiding contact with other therapists. However, in avoiding connection with the group they also managed to avoid possible feelings of envy and rivalry. As Menzies Lyth (1970) has pointed out: 'In the institutional setting it is not only the unconscious thoughts and feelings one needs to understand, but also the implicit; what is not being said.' It seemed that therapists colluded in their desire to protect the agency and to avoid spoiling the atmosphere. There seemed to be an unconscious group need to feel like a part of the ideal family.

The practice manager was also idealized. There seemed to be a collective need to idealize a good object and to keep it away from the bad object, the administrative team. As Segal (1973) has explained:

> As the processes of splitting, projection and introjection help to sort out his perceptions and emotions and divide the good from the bad, the infant feels himself to be confronted with an ideal object, which he loves and tries to acquire, keep and identify with, and a bad object, into which he has projected his aggressive impulses and which is felt to be a threat to himself and his ideal object.

However, idealization was also used as a defence against envy. As Segal suggests, 'rigid idealization may be resorted to, in an attempt to preserve some ideal object. Such idealization, however, is most precarious, since the more ideal the object, the more intense the envy' (Segal 1973).

However, there was an obvious split between the idealized organization and the administration, which was harshly denigrated. This was partly due to some incompetence on the part of the team of administrators. Messages were not passed on, files were frequently incomplete and paperwork often went missing. Referrals were thought to be unsuitable, and even though the administrators were not responsible for these, they were felt to be. However, in the role of scapegoat the administrators performed an important function for the group, for by denigrating them and projecting their destructive feelings into them counsellors avoided anxieties about their own feelings of incompetence. As Stokes (1994) has pointed out, scapegoats are very often at the boundary of the organization. In this case the receptionists and secretaries were on the boundary of the organization and the outside world. As such the administrative team seemed to be blamed for allowing the distress of the outside world, in the form of referrals, into the agency.

Similarly, feelings of hatred for the clients were also projected into the administrators, some of whom were left feeling exhausted and unsupported due to the stream of projections/projective identifications they were receiving. Denigration is a common defensive practice within institutions. As Menzies Lyth (1970) has pointed out, anxiety about one's capacity to do one's job may be 'projected downwards into subordinates and their roles'. In addition, 'the subordinates' capacities are underestimated and their roles diminished' (Menzies Lyth 1970). Finally, the least competent of the administrators was fired from the institution in the mistaken belief that this would provide a solution to the problem. Group distress often manifests itself in this way: in a great deal of blaming, between staff and management or administrators, between the agency and the outside world, between individual therapists; anyone, as long as the problem is seen as 'out there'. As Obholzer and Zagier Roberts (1994) have pointed out, many groups and organizations have a ' "difficult", "disturbed" or "impossible" member' whose behaviour is regarded as obstructive and unhelpful. This can then lead to the assumption that their removal or expulsion will solve the problems inherent in the group. 'This view is very attractive, hard to resist and tempting to act upon' (Obholzer and Zagier Roberts 1994).

Basic assumption

The group appeared to be utilizing the defensive mechanisms of projection, idealization and denigration to manage their anxiety. In addition, the basic assumption of dependency (baD) had taken over as a form of defence. Members of the group looked to the head of counselling to make decisions for them and therefore the sense of group responsibility disappeared. This state of dependency, in which nothing happened, went on for a year.

One of the other counselling organizations in the agency then won an NHS contract to provide brief psychological therapies and the Southways group discovered that the psychologists who would be providing this service would earn more than them. The envy and anxiety this engendered among group members was potent. Emotions were running high and at this point the individuals within the group attempted to defend themselves by moving from a *basic assumption of dependency* to a *basic assumption of fight-flight*, with an aggressive counterassault on the psychologists, their unsatisfactory clinical methods, and the brevity of the programme they were offering. This second basic assumption state paralysed the agency for months. Difference, dissatisfaction, envy and paranoia were now brought to the fore by the issue of inequality. Finally, a third basic assumption could also be seen in operation, the *basic assumption of pairing*, as therapists began to form small groups with other individuals whom they felt they could trust. All discussion, often centring around the superficial merits of the psychologists' approach, was confined to small groups or pairs which sabotaged the attempt of the group to address the problem.

Discussion

To operate comfortably within a group setting it is hugely important for therapists to have at least a rudimentary understanding of group dynamics. As the above example demonstrates, we need to be alert to our own blind spots: our valency for certain kinds of defences and our vulnerability to particular types of projective identification. If there is a group forum it can be helpful to explore these issues with colleagues, in the process gathering clues about the sources of some collective defences. Both personal and group therapy can also assist us to resolve these unconscious conflicts, rather than needing to do this through our work. But we do need to learn to develop the ability to observe ourselves and our reactions in order to manage and understand our own behaviour and to be able to understand and work with other group members more effectively. Hinshelwood and Skogstad (2002) suggest that we need to develop the capacity 'to identity the experiences within and around oneself while working in an institution . . . one could call it the capacity to consult oneself, a kind of internal consultant'. In the process of becoming your own internal consultant you may find it useful to ask yourself the following questions:

- What relationship do you have with the work and why?
- Why do you do this and not that in the approach that you favour?

- Why do you need to work this way and not the antithesis of this?
- Why do you imagine that you are attracted to this field and this approach and how may you be kidding yourself with your previous answer?
- How does your relationship and your feelings towards your colleagues differ (or not) from your own method of working?

Rather than seeing dissimilarity within the group as a threat and seeking solace and similarity, it is more helpful to view difference as something to be explored. We should not be afraid to brush up against the challenge of the ideological and possible intellectual dissimilarity of others. Pines conceptualizes the individual as being born into and composed from a network of others. We gain our sense of identity from the networks of our culture, politics, religion, economic and historical circumstances; each constituent part of our individual self is formed through a group experience.

As Bion suggested, knowledge about ourselves is always constituted within a group, produced within the relationship between the container and the contained – the group and the individual. Pines (1996) suggests that given that our sense of self develops through our interactions with others, it can be useful to conceptualize the self as a group. As Pines suggests, the group offers us the opportunity to connect with hidden dimensions within ourselves, the opportunity of experiencing the ways in which we are perceived by others: 'we need the others to aid in the creation and completion of ourselves, through the vision the other bestows upon us' (Pines 1996). It is only through the other that we gain a sense of ourselves; in this sense Pines proposes that 'the other can be a cause for celebration rather than for frustration and conflict'.

If we can work towards forming a mature and diverse working group, composed of individuals who can tolerate difference and diversity, we will enable our clients to bring issues of difference to the group, where they can then be worked with effectively. If the group of practitioners can model this process, then the capacity for effective work can also be possible with our clients. If the unconscious processes that affect us on both individual and organizational levels can be thought about and understood, they can be dealt with in ways that further rather than hinder development.

If we try to deny the unconscious dynamics of the group practice, the basic assumptions will be able to run unchecked, which will ultimately undermine the shared tasks of the group. In addition, as individuals working within a group, we need to be aware of regressive group defences and how we protect ourselves against levels of unspeakable distress. For example, gallows humour can act as a group defence, which can appear cathartic but can belittle and dehumanize the client group. Where clients become demonized by the projected aspects of the staff team, comments between practitioners regarding the most difficult person that one has just seen can often be heard. The power of the group to mobilize these defences can cause the group to find a common enemy. In psychotherapeutic groups this can frequently take the form of discrediting an alternative form of therapy, referrer or 'particularly difficult' client.

Where this important work is not undertaken by the group, using external support where necessary, it is more likely that workers will experience crises related to their work. These crises often occur in services in a predictable fashion: drugs workers may use substances inappropriately themselves, workers involved in sexual abuse issues may have peculiar sexual relationships themselves; and in more extreme cases some nurses may kill their patients. Carers can become persecutors if unconscious material is not worked through.

As Bion suggests, the group will only develop when it gains greater contact with reality. It is important for both group and individual to work through these anxieties by facing reality; only by working through can anxiety be mastered. The root cause of anxiety must be recognized as being located not outside but within, and this requires self-knowledge. Only then, as de Board (1978) points out, can the energy used to maintain defences be redirected to the task in hand.

References

Bion, W. R. (1968) *Experiences in Groups*, London: Tavistock.

De Board, R. (1978) *The Psychoanalysis of Organisations*, Hove and New York: Brunner-Routledge.

Freud, S. (1921) Group psychology and the analysis of the ego, *Standard Edition*, Vol. 18, London: Hogarth Press (1955).

Glickauf-Hughes, C. and Mehlman, E. (1995) Narcissistic issues in therapists: diagnostic and treatment considerations, *Psychotherapy* 32(2): 213–221.

Halton, W. (1994) Some unconscious aspects of organisational life: contributions from psychoanalysis, in A. Obholzer and V. Zagier Roberts (eds) *The Unconscious at Work: Individual and Organizational Stress in the Human Services*, Hove and New York: Brunner-Routledge.

Hinshelwood, R. D. (1985) Questions of training, *Free Associations: Psychoanalysis, Groups, Politics, Culture* 2: 7–18.

Hinshelwood, R. D. and Skogstad, W. (2002) Irradiated by distress: observing psychic pain in health-care organizations, *Psychoanalytic Psychotherapy* 16: 110–124.

Hirschhorn, L. (1985) The psychodynamics of taking the role, in A. D. Colman and M. H. A. K. Geller (eds) *Group Relations Reader 2*, Washington, WA: Rice Institute.

Menzies, I. Lyth (1970) The functioning of a social system as a defence against anxiety, *Human Relations* 11: 95–121.

Mollon, P. (1989) Anxiety, supervision and a space for thinking: some perils for clinical psychologists in learning psychotherapy, *British Journal of Medical Psychology* 62: 113–122.

Obholzer, A. and Zagier Roberts, V. (eds) (1994) *The Unconscious at Work: Individual and Organizational Stress in the Human Services*, Hove and New York: Brunner-Routledge.

Pines, M. (1996) The self as a group: the group as a self, *Group Analysis* 29: 183–190.

Racusin, G. R., Abramowitz, S. I. and Winter, W. D. (1981) Becoming a therapist: family dynamics and career choice, *Professional Psychology* 12(2): 271–279.

Raskin, R., Novacek, J. and Hogon, R. (1991) Narcissism, self-esteem and defensive self-enhancement, *Journal of Personality* 59(1): 19–38.

Segal, H. (1973) *Introduction to the work of Melanie Klein*, London: Hogarth Press.

Stokes, J. (1994) Institutional chaos and personal stress, in A. Obholzer and V. Zagier Roberts (eds) *The Unconscious at Work: Individual and Organizational Stress in the Human Services*, Hove and New York: Brunner-Routledge.

Vaillant, G. E. and Vaillant, C. O. (1990) Natural history of male psychological health, XII: a 45-year study of predictors of successful aging at 65, *American Journal of Psychiatry* 147: 31–37.

Wolfenstein, E. V. (1990) Group phantasies and the individual. A critical analysis of psychoanalytic group psychology, *Free Associations* 20: 150–180.

Zagier Roberts, V. (1994) The self-assigned impossible task, in A. Obholzer and V. Zagier Roberts (eds) *The Unconscious at Work: Individual and Organizational Stress in the Human Services*, Hove and New York: Brunner-Routledge.

Chapter 7

Psychodynamic counselling and complementary therapy

Towards an effective collaboration

Robert Withers

Introduction

The term complementary therapy conjures up an image of acupuncturists, osteopaths and homeopaths happily collaborating with doctors and counsellors in an integrated health care setting for the benefit of their clients. Sadly, though perhaps not altogether surprisingly, the reality is usually somewhat different – especially in private practice. As a flood of counsellors and complementary therapists (CTs) graduates from private colleges and university courses, practitioners are forced to compete for the limited number of clients willing and able to afford the cost of treatment. Such are the dynamics of the marketplace that even those therapists lucky enough to work in a successful independent clinic tend to operate in splendid isolation. Nobody pays a private practitioner to consult with colleagues. Cross-referrals are therefore relatively few and often inappropriate, understanding of other modalities is limited, and creative interchange between practitioners is rare – in what is essentially a protectionist situation. Meanwhile waiting lists often run into years for those patients 'lucky' enough to be referred to a counsellor or complementary therapist for the severely limited services available within the statutory sector.

It is surprising perhaps, given the ironies and injustices of this situation, that any collaboration between CTs and counsellors is possible at all, especially in the private sector. But there is an additional series of implicit conceptual clashes that further complicates this essentially economic conflict of interests. These focus around opposing models of symptom causation and cure.

In complementary therapy, as Kaptchuk (2001) and others have convincingly demonstrated, disease is nearly always regarded as emanating from some sort of imbalance in the 'vital force'. This force is conceptualized as lying behind both the physical expressions of the body and the psychological phenomena of the mind. In this sense complementary therapy promotes itself as 'holistic' and opposed to the dualism that underpins modern culture's polarization of physical and mental illness. In a philosophical sense we could therefore characterize it as advocating a kind of 'dual aspect theory' (see e.g. Young 1990). That is, mind and body are both regarded as aspects of some single underlying substance – in this case a vital energy or field.

In contrast, psychodynamic counselling does not offer a challenge to Cartesian dualism; and this is probably one important reason that it has been more readily accepted by modern medicine. It is a psychological therapy offering to treat disorders of the mind. By and large it leaves treatment of the body to the physicians. Where it does treat the body, it does so by purely psychological means. Its theories of somatization may pose a radical challenge to conventional conceptions of mind and of mind–body interaction, involving as they do the notion of the unconscious. They also clearly imply an expanded view of the mind's area of influence. But to utilize Wittgenstein's (1958) metaphor, they do not challenge the basic rules of the different 'language games'. Orthodox medicine can continue to use the rules of the scientific language game to talk about the body, while psychotherapists can continue to use the rules of the psychological language game to talk about the mind. It may be possible to dispute the best game from within which to articulate the aetiology and treatment of a particular patient, but the games themselves remain intact. CT, with its notion of the vital force, in contrast challenges the rules by undermining the very distinction between the games.

As I hope to show later, this conceptual clash can have profound consequences that affect attempts at collaboration. But before going on to look at this in more detail I would like first to describe my own journey from complementary therapy to psychotherapy and out of that to raise a few initial questions.

From complementary therapy to psychotherapy – a personal journey

My early trainings in complementary medicine gave me an excellent understanding of the principles of acupuncture and homeopathy, but only a limited understanding of western medicine, and very little clinical experience. So the transition from classroom to consulting room came as something of a shock. I was expected to take responsibility for real people – often with complex and serious health problems – as the following case illustrates.

An early case

Jon was a 20-year-old university student. Following a medical examination and blood tests, his doctor had suggested a diagnosis of Hodgkin's lymphoma, a potentially fatal cancer of the lymph glands. All that was needed to verify this diagnosis was a biopsy. However, Jon refused to undergo the necessary surgical procedure, stating that in his opinion it carried an unacceptable health risk and that if the biopsy were positive he would refuse orthodox treatment anyway. I was in the final stages of my training when he asked me for homeopathic treatment. I tried to encourage him to reconsider his position and have the biopsy but he was adamant that he would not, so I attempted to master my unease and agreed to take him on. The situation was further complicated by the fact that Jon was a close friend. I knew I was taking a risk treating him. What if it didn't work and he died? On the other hand homeopaths were scarce in the mid-1970s in Britain and no more experienced colleague was available to refer him on to, even if he had been open to this suggestion and able to afford it. Quite apart from my own need for more clinical experience then, I found myself wondering how I would feel if I didn't treat him and he died. So with Jon's active participation in the process, I compiled an exhaustive list of all his symptoms and duly prescribed lycopodium 200 in accordance with classical homeopathic principles. Over a period of about a year, we watched as the lumps on his neck first receded then disappeared and his general health improved. He remains well to this day.

Reflection

Although this story has a happy ending, it immediately highlights a number of issues. Perhaps the most obvious of these concerns boundaries. From a counselling perspective of course the case illustrates my shocking lack of awareness of the importance of boundaries at the time. Some of this shock results no doubt from differing attitudes to the body within counselling and complementary therapy – a crucial point to which I will return later. In addition to this however, it is fair to say that no self-respecting counsellor would agree to treat a friend, let alone one with such a life-threatening condition. Quite apart from the risks to the patient, the emotional strain on the therapist would be considered unacceptable and the distortions imposed on the therapeutic relationship likely to render effective treatment impossible.

From a complementary therapy point of view, however, the situation is not quite so clear-cut. Unlike the counsellor, the CT is of course expected to treat physical symptoms. It is also not uncommon, especially for newly qualified practitioners or those in training, to gain therapeutic experience by treating friends and relatives for free. In a similar way the early pioneers of psychoanalysis used to analyse one another's dreams (Jung 1963) and it is not unknown, even today, for counsellors to use friends to meet training requirements for case material. But not withstanding these occasional lapses, it is fair to say that boundaries that seem self-evident to counsellors and psychotherapists can by no means be taken for granted by complementary therapists. It is common practice for CTs, in contrast to counsellors, to treat friends and relatives of existing patients professionally, in much the same way as a family doctor, for example. While this might not matter in CT, the real knowledge that patient and practitioner already had of one another could undermine the crucial role of fantasy and unconscious fantasy (phantasy) in the evolution of the transference and countertransference within counselling.

Of course today, with homeopaths flooding the marketplace, I would easily be able to refer a friend in Jon's position to a colleague. Nevertheless, I cannot be sure that I would not behave in exactly the same way in the same situation. The only practical alternative to my treating him was no treatment. Most boundaries are context related rather than self-evident or universal; and when practitioners forget this, problems can arise. A CT might, for instance, divulge inappropriate information about a counsellor if they are unaware of the role of ph/fantasy in psychodynamic counselling. A counsellor might then condemn such a CT for keeping 'sloppy' boundaries if judged by their own standards. Simple problems like this can easily undermine mutual respect and disrupt effective cross-referral and collaboration. However, quite apart from this issue of boundaries, there is another question that links back to the conceptual clash outlined in the introduction: 'What made Jon well?'

Questions about causality in medicine are notoriously hard to answer. Healing often seems to have something of an element of mystery about it. As the philosopher David Hume (2000) famously remarked, the whole issue of the apparently 'necessary connection' between a cause and its effect is deeply problematic. Nevertheless, both Jon and I felt pretty confident that the conventional homeo-pathic explanation of the remedy's effects was the most likely. On this account the vital force in the remedy (liberated by the process of homeopathic potentization) had interacted with Jon's own 'vital field' in such a way as to restore his health. The process was equivalent to immunization except that it operated on an 'ener-getic' rather than material level. We didn't worry that conven-tional science had been unable to confirm the existence of such a vital force. We assumed that this was due to the inadequacies of its investigations to date and that it was only a matter of time before more subtle experiments demonstrated the truth of what homeo-paths had been saying for years. In fact I was personally involved at the time in a series of 'ground-breaking' experiments at the University of Sussex that aimed to use 'Kirlian photography' to prove just this. A group of Soviet researchers (Ostrander and Schroeder 1971) claimed to have succeeded in photographing the human 'energy field' using the technique, while a group of British researchers (Milner and Smart 1975) claimed to have photo-graphed the vital energy of homeopathic remedies. And I was attempting to verify their findings.

It was with a growing sense of disappointment, however, that I came to realize that these researchers had not demonstrated the reality of the vital force at all. In fact they had merely succeeded in presenting a series of poorly controlled experiments as sensational findings, while ignoring perfectly plausible conventional explana-tions for their results. I was faced with a dilemma: either I could continue with my experiments and publish these negative findings or abandon my research. I chose the latter and in so doing gained first-hand experience of what is known as 'positive publication bias'. Researchers tend to publish positive findings in preference to negative ones and this creates a bias in the literature.

Perhaps this was a mistake. I still read accounts that claim Kirlian photography has demonstrated the existence of the vital force in complementary medicine (Vithoulkas 1980; Whitmont 1996). In general they refer back to the same old discredited literature. But I had had considerable first-hand experience of the positive effects of both homeopathy and acupuncture by this time and was too intrigued to find out how they worked to waste more time and effort researching up a blind alley.

Returning to the question of what had made Jon (and the people like him) well, I realized that if something physically real was at work, even as just one aspect of the 'vital force', then homeopathic remedies should perform better than placebos in a double-blind trial. But a literature search revealed no relevant well-controlled studies. Since then there have been a number of double-blind trials on homeopathy and interestingly none have yielded unequivocally positive results despite the aforementioned positive publication bias (Ernst 2002; Shang 2005). Nor have there been any repeatable, well-designed experiments demonstrating a physical mechanism for homeopathy's effects to date. On the other hand, the limited number of studies that compare homeopathy's effects to other medical interventions in a variety of conditions have generally been positive (Mathie 2003; Dean 2004).

So although homeopathy appears to work, the evidence seems to suggest that the chances of finding a physical explanation for its effects are fairly slim. And theoretical considerations render these even more remote. It is possible to use Avogadro's theorem to calculate the number of molecules present in a particular homeopathic pill. This revealed that the chances of finding a single molecule of lycopodium in Jon's 'potentized' remedy were several billion to one against.

But if homeopathy's effects are not physically induced, could they be caused psychologically? If such an account should prove possible, then this would certainly seem to offer an advantage on the basis of Occam's razor over the more esoteric 'vital force' hypothesis of complementary therapy. But it is at this point that the conceptual clash between psychodynamics and complementary therapy begins to bite. CTs tend to offer accounts of sickness and recovery that seem inherently implausible and paradoxically materialistic to both scientists and psychodynamic therapists, while psychodynamic accounts of the same phenomena can seem implausibly psychological and unnecessarily blinkered to CTs.

Over the years I have continued to search for an understanding of homeopathy's effects. But in the absence of any plausible physical explanation, I began to review my own cases with the possibility of finding a psychological one. When I did so I realized that patients sometimes seemed to get worse despite my 'good' prescribing, and better despite my 'poor' prescribing. Choosing a remedy that mirrored my patient's symptom picture accurately certainly seemed to help, but this was by no means the only relevant factor. The ability of both my homeopathic and acupuncture patients to express meaningful emotion in sessions, especially around significant events that coincided with the onset of their symptoms, seemed an important indicator of therapeutic outcome. Leaving aside those people who were never going to get any better, the quality of their relationship with me also appeared to be relevant. Put simply, those people who had a good feeling about me tended to get better. Those who had a difficulty with me often did not (see Withers 2001). Looking back, I can see that the positive quality of Jon's relationship with me was probably a significant factor in his recovery. I also realized that the onset of his symptoms coincided with the painful break-up of a relationship with a longstanding girlfriend. Numerous researchers have commented on similar links between life events and the onset of illness (Taylor 1987; Cohen and Herbert 1996).

Around the same time as beginning these clinical reflections, I discovered Herbert Silberer (1917) and Carl Jung's (1943) work on alchemy. They argued that the alchemists had projected the contents of their own unconscious into the substances they worked with. As these physical substances were transformed, so were they – via the symbolic transformation of these projected unconscious contents. I wondered if it was possible that something analogous was happening with homeopathy. If patients projected their unconscious complexes into homeopathic remedies, could taking them in potentized, detoxified form somehow have therapeutic consequences (Withers 1979)? After many more years of clinical practice as both a homeopath and psychotherapist, I was finally able to articulate this in a form I was happy with (Withers 2001, 2003). I will attempt to articulate this later in relation to Jon's recovery.

Meanwhile, at this relatively early stage in my career I had already begun to feel that psychological factors were far more important than I had previously realized. Paradoxically, despite most homeopaths insistence on the potency of the vital force, there is a strong strand within homeopathy itself that contends that illness comes from the psyche or 'inner man' (Kent 1911). But if my complementary therapy training had left me with only a limited understanding of western medicine, it had been even more inadequate in equipping me to understand and work with these largely unconscious psychological factors. It was at this point that I decided to train to be an analytical psychotherapist and attempt to work with these forces in a more ethical and effective manner.

Observations concerning complementary therapists

It might be pertinent to pause at this point and attempt to draw together a few observations for counsellors wishing to work collaboratively with CTs in an independent setting. Of course complementary therapy has become more widely accepted since I trained and most of the trainings are more broadly based and professionally set up. The change of name from alternative to complementary therapy has also been helpful insofar as it indicates a genuine desire to work more cooperatively with other disciplines. Nevertheless, it is worth bearing in mind that many of the anxieties and insecurities that beset me still apply today and may militate against effective collaboration.

The first anxiety I noted affects counsellors as well as CTs and concerns *making a living*. If anything this pressure is worse today, given the increased competition for patients mentioned in the introduction. There is no easy solution to this, but the anxiety could be addressed along psychodynamic lines. If it is consciously acknowledged rather than denied, it is less likely to be acted out defensively in ways that disrupt communication and cooperation. In addition, it is helpful here if both counsellor and CT can establish jointly recognized limits of competence, so that they minimize the risk of poaching from one another. This is not always easy to do though because, as we have already seen, accounts of aetiology and cure sometimes rival rather than complement one another. Not only this, but competence is affected by individual factors such as personality and experience, not just the discipline practised. So to a certain extent it probably needs to be flexibly negotiated between individual practitioners. On the other hand, there is clearly also a need for the development of a more general interdisciplinary code of ethics and practice to establish rough limits of competence between the different professions – where this is possible.

Another anxiety concerns responsibility for the treatment of physical symptoms. There is a large amount of research that suggests connections between psychological conflict and physical or psychosomatic symptoms (Alexander 1950; Weiner 1973; Taylor 1987). Nevertheless, it is highly unlikely that patients with physical symptoms – certainly ones as severe or potentially life threatening as Jon's – will give a psychodynamic therapist primary responsibility for treatment of those symptoms. Such patients do however constitute a significant part of the CTs practice. But the vast majority of CTs in private practice are not medically qualified, so they carry high levels of anxiety about their responsibility for these patients. I have certainly found myself wishing I had a medical qualification at times and feeling like a quack or a fraud without it. Under these circumstances, I nearly always try to work cooperatively with the patient's doctor, but have no doubt lost clients because of this apparent lack of confidence. It is not uncommon, however, for CTs to react defensively to these anxieties and denigrate orthodox medicine while omnipotently elevating their own healing powers. This is especially seductive when patients share this denigration and idealize the CT. The potential for a dynamic like this can be clearly seen in my interaction with Jon. Perhaps if I had been more conscious of this at the time, I would have challenged his refusal to consider conventional treatment more vigorously.

Analogously, CTs often feel anxious about the responsibility of working with their patient's emotional/psychological issues without counselling qualifications. Here too reactions vary. Among the CTs I have supervised, the most common reaction is to want to refer a client on to a counsellor the minute an emotional issue surfaces. In this way the client is given the implicit message that the practitioner is uncomfortable with emotions and learns to inhibit their expression. As a result an important therapeutic opportunity can be lost. In addition, the patient, who may be suffering from a problem that presents physically but is reinforced emotionally, is unlikely to be able to see the relevance of and use the counselling referral. At the opposite extreme is the CT who reacts to these anxieties by mobilizing omnipotent defences and imagining that their own therapeutic intervention is all that is needed to resolve even the most extreme cases of emotional conflict and trauma. Such a practitioner is unlikely to be able to ask for help even when it is needed and becomes vulnerable to work-related burn-out and various forms of acting out. Under these circumstances the CT usually needs effective personal therapy before being able to work cooperatively with a psychodynamic counsellor at all.

Fortunately, however, there are a growing number of CTs who can realistically recognize the limits of their own competence. These practitioners may request psychodynamic supervision for their more difficult cases or, where appropriate, make a referral on to a counsellor. In my experience it is often possible under these circumstances for the counsellor and CT to continue working with the same patient. And it can smack of omnipotence for either party to insist otherwise. Of course there is a danger of the client splitting feelings between practitioners, but it is usually possible to work with this (Withers 2003). Some CT clients eventually reach a point where they recognize the underlying emotional nature of their problems and move on altogether from CT to psychodynamic counselling or psychotherapy. There are also certain clients who make the reverse journey. In these circumstances the problem of splitting is less likely to arise.

Before closing this brief section, I would like to make what amounts to a plea for tolerance towards CTs. They may sometimes seem like arrogant, money-grabbing, new age charlatans with a magical world view, but they are also often dedicated professionals attempting to offer a service to the many patients who do not fit neatly into either the purely physical or purely mental illness categories. They work without the secure base of a generally accepted world view, without the professional recognition or status of either doctors or psychotherapists, and often without these colleagues' respect. Counsellors and other therapists wishing to work collaboratively with them should not be surprised if they sometimes act defensively under these circumstances.

The body in psychodynamic therapy

There is a general supposition that permeates through into popular culture (see e.g. Hustvedt 2003) that the classical hysteric, that once beloved patient of traditional psychoanalysis, has mysteriously disappeared since Freud's day. However, in his book *Hysteria* (2000) Christopher Bollas questions this. He believes that the hysterical patient is merely in hiding. In psychoanalysis she often ends up being wrongly diagnosed as suffering from either

'borderline' (Bion 1962) or 'false self' (Winni
He refers approvingly to Elaine Showalter's boo
in which she argues convincingly that our cultu
denigration of psychological disturbance can result
patients presenting themselves as suffering from a serie
ently physical disorders. These range from ME or chronic
syndrome, through Gulf War syndrome, to a variety of com
complaints such as headache, backache and insomnia. These a
of course, the very patients who tend to end up presenting themselves to complementary therapists. The irony of this situation is
that if Bollas and Showalter are right, then the people psychoanalysis evolved in order to treat have ended up avoiding it. They
go instead to practitioners less well trained to treat them who tend
to collude with the view that their suffering is physical or 'ener-
getic'. Despite the 'Freudian revolution', our culture clearly still
has difficulty even accepting the reality of the psyche – let alone
asserting the dignity of those who suffer from a psychological
disturbance.

How has the hysteric's infidelity to the psychoanalyst come
about? I believe that a part of the answer can be found within the
history of psychoanalysis itself. When Freud began treating
hysterics towards the end of the nineteenth century, they had only
recently been regarded as possessed by evil spirits (Foucault 1988;
Hustvedt 2003). Freud, of course, challenged this view by looking
for the sense in their symptoms. He operated with a model and a
method that was remarkably similar in many respects to that
employed by present day holistic practitioners. On the practical
side he was not afraid to touch his patients. He hypnotized them
by applying pressure to their foreheads and asked them to recall
the traumatic events that underlay both their bodily and psychological symptoms. On the theoretical side, his notion of 'libido'
has been understandably criticized for being too firmly based in
the metaphors of nineteenth-century hydraulics. But in its favour it
did at least have a solid physicality alongside its more psychological side; and it is remarkably reminiscent of complementary
therapy's vital force, which attempts the same job of uniting the
mind/body divide. In addition, his early works such as 'The
Project' (Freud 1895) clearly intend to formulate a therapeutic
model that integrates psychology with neurology.

It was only after Freud had observed Anna O's erotic attachment
to his colleague Joseph Breuer (Freud and Breuer 1893) and

ic transferences to himself (see
g his patients. Around the same
:ory (based on a trauma model)
neurosis (see Jones 1961); and
gical therapy was born. It seems
integrated mind/body therapy
:, Freud succumbed to a com-
personal pressures (see Masson
umably relates to the fear of
ble erotic transference/counter-
ıral side, it is as if our society is
chological power in the same
ıd therefore impels us towards
one side or other of the divide. Perhaps this arises from collective
fear of losing the hard-won freedoms that go with separating
church from state and science from religion. (Descartes 1984–91).
Or perhaps Freud's radicalism just waned with his youth.

Whatever the cause, subsequent theoretical developments within
psychoanalysis have tended to add to this alienation from the
body. With the demise of the hysteric, came the rise of the
borderline personality and of the false self. These diagnoses and
others like them place the body in a far less accessible area of the
person, and liken psychosomatic to psychotic states, where early
damage in the capacity to symbolize is hypothesized (Winnicott
1949; Bion 1962; Taylor 1987). These developments may have
added valuable techniques such as the use of the countertransference and projective identification in psychotherapy. But arguably, they have also contributed to the alienation of those suffering
psychologically influenced physical symptoms, including hysteria,
from psychoanalysis and driven them towards the CTs.

Patrick Pietroni, a respected colleague and former mentor of
mine, used to tell a Mulla Nasrudin story that can be used to
illustrate a related point (Shah 1983):

> One day Nasrudin [a sort of holy fool] was spotted by a
> neighbour on his hands and knees under a street light outside
> his house.
> 'What are you doing here?' asked the neighbour.
> 'Looking for my key', replied the Mulla.
> 'Where did you lose it?' asked the neighbour, getting down on
> his hands and knees to help.

'Inside the house'.
'Then why are you looking out here?'
'Because it's brighter!' answered Nasrudin.

There are supposed to be seven different levels of meaning in these Nasrudin tales. But I am concerned with the one that goes something like this – though you can probably already guess it. For the psychologically orientated analysts – the later Freud, the object relations and attachment therapists, etc. – the streetlight is like the mind but the key has been lost in the darkness (unconscious) of the hysterical or psychosomatic patient's bodily symptom. For the more physically orientated CTs and body therapists, the streetlight is like the body, but the patient needs to look in the darkness of the psyche to find the key that might free them from their symptoms. We are all, like Nasrudin, in danger of looking in the area that we know about but failing to find what we seek as a result.

Towards reintegration

Conceptual collaboration

Despite this danger, I do believe that it is possible for orthodox psychodynamic therapists to work effectively with emotionally influenced bodily symptoms. But I also believe that there is an analytic culture that tends to resist the body and blind us to the meaning of its symptoms and sensations (both our own and the client's). I have certainly found it far harder to effect symptomatic relief of bodily symptoms with psychotherapy than with complementary therapy. Some of the reasons for this will be clear from the above considerations. But paradoxically, the very theories that alienate analytic patients from the body, by equating psychosomatic with psychotic symptoms, can help offer a plausible explanation for homeopathy's relative success with them.

Bion (1962) found that working analytically with such 'psychotic' parts of a patient's personality entails paying special attention to the countertransference and in particular to the process of projective identification. Toxic, symptom-producing parts of the patient's experience, including unmanageable emotions, become forced into the analyst. If the analyst is able to contain these and use his 'reverie' to detoxify them, they can eventually be safely returned to the patient through analytic interpretation. They can then be thought about, symbolized in words or dreams and generally reintegrated by the patient. Bion thought of this as a process of transformation of toxic, symptom-producing beta elements into detoxified alpha elements.

The parallels with homeopathy are uncanny, except that here the remedy rather than the analyst, acts as a container (see the remarks on alchemy earlier). The homeopathic process of potentization (dilution and succussion of the remedy), rather than the analyst's reverie, acts as the transformer of beta into alpha elements. Swallowing the remedy is then the symbolic equivalent (Segal 1957) of taking in the analyst's verbal interpretations. But since the whole process is happening in homeopathy without being consciously acknowledged, it can bypass some of the patient's resistances – thus relieving related physical symptoms more quickly.

Applying all this to Jon now, let us assume that unmanageable feelings about his failed love affair were acting as toxic beta elements to his psyche-soma. Perhaps in this form they were somehow undermining the efficiency of his immune system (Taylor 1987) and contributing to his Hodgkin's disease – if that is what he really had. At any rate he 'knew' he was taking the safe form of a substance that could produce his symptoms in a healthy state, along the lines of the homeopathic principle of treating like with like. But if he also knew on an unconscious level that his split off grief was contributing to his condition, it was a small step for him to imagine he was internalizing a detoxified safe version of that grief when he swallowed his remedy. Containment and symptom relief could follow without him ever having to consciously fully experience the frighteningly crazy feelings associated with his failed love affair. And the whole process could take place without the necessity of any physical effect from the lycopodium.

Interestingly, lycopodium is made from the spoors of a moss that relies on a symbiotic fungus to provide its water and nutrition (Gutman 1974). If this association to the life cycle of lycopodium is regarded as the equivalent of the analyst's reverie, it may offer a clue to lycopodium's special capacity to act as a symbolic container for the unmanageable symbiotic parts of Jon's personality following his failed love affair.

Of course it is usually impossible to know for sure exactly what makes any particular patient well. Perhaps Jon would have got better in time anyway. But if the lycopodium did influence his recovery, an interesting piece of research by Noel Pratt (1971) lends weight to the argument that it was psychological rather than physical factors that produced its effects.

Homeopathic medicines are prescribed on the basis of their ability to produce the same symptoms in a healthy person that the patient is suffering from. Taking a potential remedy in a healthy state and noting the physical and psychological symptoms it produces is known as 'proving' it. Once a remedy picture is produced in this way it can be used in a diluted (potentized) form to treat someone suffering from the same symptoms. But homeopathic provings are traditionally done without any placebo controls or blinding. In other words, the prover knows what he or she is taking and this knowledge is likely to influence the symptom picture produced. Lycopodium powder had been in use prior to homeopathy as a coating to keep pills dry and was believed to be medically inert. In a case such as this, provings are performed with the remedy in a potentized state; since potentization was believed to release its dormant medical powers.

In a paper that refreshingly bucks the trend towards positive publication bias, Noel Pratt conducted a double-blind proving on lycopodium and concluded that those proving potentized lycopodium were no more likely to produce a lycopodium symptom picture than those taking a placebo. It seems likely therefore that the symptom picture produced by those originally proving lycopodium reflected those symptoms they believed were produced by the remedy rather than any physical effect of the remedy itself. Clearly there is significant scope for the operation of factors such as suggestion and unconscious association both here and in other traditional homeopathic provings. So a non-blind prover taking lycopodium who knows about its symbiotic fungus might attribute feelings of grief and anxiety when alone as well as a variety of digestive symptoms to taking it. Other features such as lycopodium powder's dryness and propensity to ignite with a flash when struck hard could lead to further elements of its symptom picture through a similar process of association and suggestion (see e.g. Whitmont 1980 for a fuller consideration of the lycopodium symptom picture). Once a remedy picture has been built up in this way, taking it can effect symptom relief through a combination of its capacity to act as a symbolic container for detoxified beta elements and simple suggestion.

Having briefly sketched out the possibility for a conceptual collaboration that helps explain the therapeutic effects of homeopathy in this way, I will conclude with a clinical example of collaboration. (I refer readers wishing to investigate this conceptual collaboration further to Withers 2001, 2003.)

Clinical collaboration through supervision

Chris was a complementary therapist who had trained in a form of bodywork that utilizes touch and movement to treat a variety of conditions. He had recently started the university course I teach, exploring the psychodynamics of the therapeutic relationship for body workers and practitioners of complementary therapy. He had no other specialist psychological training. His client 'Anne' was suffering from chronic back pain, and had had several years of psychotherapeutic treatment that had proved very useful without having any lasting effect on her physical symptoms. When Chris placed his hands under the affected area of her back, he could sense significant muscular tension and asked, 'Why do you think you are holding on to your pelvis?'

At first Anne could not answer, but as Chris encouraged her to relax her muscles she replied, 'My father always told us "Good is not good enough, you can always do better, you must always succeed".'

'So perhaps you are just pulling your waist together to look thinner?' he said, attempting to soften his question with a laugh.

'Well you could be right,' replied Anne. She began to cry, going on to speak shamefully about a time when she had been anorexic. While she cried, Chris noticed that she remained in control of her body despite the loss of emotional control. Her pelvis stayed stuck in a contracted state. In (group) supervision Chris bravely reported the following dream:

> Several nights after the consultation, I dreamed I was having sex with Anne. The remarkable thing about this dream was that whilst having sex, we were engaged in animated non-sexual conversation, and I remember thinking that Anne was not at all feeling what we were doing. The situation felt oddly casual. Our conversation and our physical movements were completely unrelated.

No doubt this dream says something about Chris, and also the state of the therapeutic relationship. In the supervision group we chose to focus on what it might be saying about Anne, however. From this angle the dream could be treated diagnostically – as confirmation of her emotional disconnection from her body. In it their conversation was entirely divorced from their bodily actions, just as Anne's sobs had been cut off from her pelvis in the preceding session (an example of the mind/body dissociation so common in our post-Cartesian culture). This diagnostic insight, which arose from Chris's reflection about the dream, crucially informed the rest of Anne's treatment, which eventually achieved a degree of physical symptom relief not afforded by psychotherapy alone. And Anne, who had been in a committed relationship for many years, actually became pregnant shortly after the reported consultation.

Conclusion

In this chapter I have outlined some of the opportunities for and obstacles to collaboration between complementary and psychodynamic therapists in private practice. I have suggested that there are potential conceptual and economic rivalries between the two disciplines. I have used homeopathy to illustrate some of these conceptual rivalries. In particular I have argued that therapeutic effects attributed within homeopathy to the vital force could be due to the operation of largely unconscious psychological factors. I have not had space to consider other complementary therapies, but although physical factors may play a larger part in their effects than homeopathy, they too generally play down the importance of psychological factors, which are nevertheless likely to be appreciable.

In addition I have used my personal experience to illustrate some of the anxieties carried by CTs and have suggested that these can interfere with effective collaboration if not acknowledged and adequately contained. I have also outlined some of the reasons for my own move out of complementary medicine into psychodynamic/analytic therapy, though these may well have unconscious determinants of which I am only dimly aware.

While complementary therapy tends to emphasize the importance of a quasi-physical vital force, psychoanalysis tends to underplay the importance of the body and of bodily symptoms –

despite its origins in a more holistic paradigm. This has tended to discourage a large number of patients who identify themselves as suffering from physical symptoms from consulting with psychodynamic therapists, even though those symptoms may be maintained by emotional factors. Such patients are more likely to consult CTs who are however less capable of dealing with the emotional components in their complaints.

In my final section I have returned to the issue of homeopathy. In particular I have attempted to use the insights of Wilfred Bion to open up a potentially fruitful area of conceptual collaboration with psychodynamic therapy. This may feel like a dismissal of homeopathy to those who mistakenly regard the physical as the limit to the real. I prefer to regard it as a relocation of homeopathy within the psychological language game, which is the richer because of this, especially in terms of conceptualizing the mind's influence upon the body.

I have concluded with an example of psychodynamic supervision that illustrates some of the potential for fruitful clinical collaboration between the disciplines.

References

Alexander, F. (1950) *Psychosomatic Medicine: Its Principles and Applications*, New York: Norton.

Bion, W. (1962) *Learning from Experience*, London: Heinemann.

Bollas, C. (2000) *Hysteria*, London and New York: Routledge.

Cohen, S. and Herbert, T. B. (1996) Health psychology: psychological factors and physical disease from the perspective of human psychoneuroimmunology, *Annual Review of Psychology* 47: 113–142.

Dean, M. E. (2004) *The Trials of Homeopathy: Origins, Structure and Development*, Essen: KVC and Verlag.

Descartes, R. (1984–91 [1641]) *The Philosophical Writings of Descartes* (J. Cottingham, R. Stoothoff, D. Murdoch and A. Kenny Ed. and Trans.), Cambridge: Cambridge University Press.

Ernst, E. (2002) A systematic review of systematic reviews of homoeopathy, *British Journal of Clinical Pharmacology* 54(6): 577.

Foucault, M. (1988) *Madness and Civilization: A History of Insanity in the Age of Reason*, London: Vintage.

Freud, S. (1895) Project for a scientific psychology, *Standard Edition* Vol. 1, London: Hogarth Press.

Freud, S. and Breuer, J. (1893–6) Studies on hysteria, *Standard Edition* Vol. 2, London: Hogarth Press.

Gutman, W. (1974) Lycopodium, *Journal of the American Institute of Homeopathy* June: 73–79.

Hume, D. (2000 [1739]) *A Treatise of Human Nature*, Oxford: Oxford Philosophical Texts.

Hustvedt, S. (2003) *What I Loved*, London: Hodder and Stoughton, p. 54.

Jones, E. (1961) *The Life and Works of Sigmund Freud*, New York: Basic Books.

Jung, C. (1943) Psychology and alchemy, *Collected Works*, Vol. 12, London: Routledge and Kegan Paul (1953).

—— (1963) *Memories, Dreams and Reflections*, London: Collins and Routledge Kegan Paul.

Kaptchuk, T. (2001) Historical context of the concept of vitalism in complementary and alternative medicine, in M. Micozzi (ed.) *Fundamentals of Complementary and Alternative Medicine*, 3rd edn, Edinburgh: Churchill Livingstone.

Kent, J. (1911) *Lectures on Homeopathic Philosophy*, Philadelphia: Boericke and Tafel.

Masson, J. (1984) *The Assault on Truth*, New York: Farrar, Straus and Giroux.

Mathie, R. (2003) *The Research Evidence Base for Homeopathy: A Fresh Assessment of the Literature*, www.sciencedirect.com.

Milner, N. and Smart, T. (1975) *The Loom of Creation*, London: Spearman.

Ostrander, S. and Schroeder, L. (1971) *Psychic Discoveries Behind the Iron Curtain*, New York: Bantam.

Pratt, N. (1971) Double blind trials by medical students, *British Homoeopathic Journal* 60(1): 41.

Segal, H. (1957) Notes on symbol formation, in H. Segal *The Work of Hannah Segal*, London: Free Association.

Shah, I. (1983) *The Exploits of the Incomparable Mulla Nasrudin*, London: Octagon.

Shang, A. (2005) Are the clinical effects of homoeopathy placebo effects? Comparative study of placebo-controlled trials of homoeopathy and allopathy, *Lancet* 366(9487): 726–732.

Showalter, E. (1997) *Hystories*, New York: Columbia University Press.

Silberer, H. (1917/1971) *The Hidden Symbolism of Alchemy and the Occult Arts* (F. Jelliffe Trans.), New York: Dover.

Taylor, G. (1987) *Psychosomatic Medicine and Contemporary Psychoanalysis*, Madison, CT: IUP.

Vithoulkas, G. (1980) *The Science of Homeopathy*, New York: Grove Press.

Weiner, H. (1973) *Psychobiology and Human Disease*, New York: Elsevier.

Whitmont, E. (1996) Alchemy, homeopathy and the treatment of borderline cases, *Journal of Analytical Psychology* 41: 369–386.

—— (1980) *Psyche and Substance*, Richmond, CA: North Atlantic Books.

Winnicott, D. (1942) Child department consultations, *International Journal of Psychoanalysis* 23. Also in *Through Paediatrics to Psychoanalysis*, London: Hogarth Press (1987).

—— (1949) Mind and its relation to the psyche-soma, *International Journal of Psychoanalysis*. Also in *Through Paediatrics to Psychoanalysis*, London: Hogarth Press (1987).

Withers, R. (1979) Towards a psychology of homoeopathy and the high potencies, *British Homoeopathic Journal* 68(3).

—— (2001) Psychoanalysis, complementary medicine and the placebo, in D. Peters (ed.) *Understanding the Placebo Effect in Complementary Medicine*, Edinburgh: Churchill Livingstone.

—— (ed.) (2003) *Controversies in Analytical Psychology*, Hove and New York: Brunner-Routledge.

Wittgenstein, L. (1958) *Philosophical Investigations*, Oxford: Blackwell.

Young, R. (1990) The mind–body problem, in R. C. Olby (ed.) *Companion to the History of Modern Science*, London and New York: Routledge.

Chapter 8

Working from home in independent practice

Rosalind Field

Introduction

Traditionally counsellors have worked from home. Some use their home as their sole workplace while others also work for an agency and supplement their income by working from home on a part-time basis. The very nature of working from home introduces a new context to the therapeutic work and creates dynamics peculiar to it. These dynamics not only affect the work between counsellor and client, but may also extend to other family members, friends and neighbours with positive and negative consequences.

In order to set the scene for this chapter I look briefly at the history of counsellors and psychotherapists working from home. I explore the main advantages and disadvantages to the counsellor and the client, and how the work may be affected by the fact that it takes place in the counsellor's home. In particular I look at boundary issues and how these may be more vulnerable to becoming blurred when working in this context. I also discuss the kind of work accommodation required and how this may create conflict if we share our home with others. As there is little in the literature on the subject, I explore in more depth how working from home affects and is affected by the counsellor's family relationships, giving examples from my own experience. I make particular reference to the way that envy plays an important part in these relationships. I explore issues of confidentiality and finally issues of safety for both counsellor and client.

History

Traditionally psychotherapists in independent practice have worked from home. Psychoanalysis, the precursor to psychotherapy and counselling, was brought to the UK by Freud via Ernest Jones, one of Freud's analysands in 1913. Freud himself came to live in the UK the year before he died in 1939 and worked from his home in Maresfield Gardens in London up until a few weeks before his death.

Although, like Freud, Jones was medically qualified, he supported Freud's belief that it is not necessary to have a medical qualification in order to practise psychoanalysis. Indeed, Freud's daughter Anna was not medically qualified and became an influential lay psychoanalyst in her own right. Consequently when Jones founded the British Psychoanalytic Society in 1924 many of its members were lay practitioners. Therefore, unlike in the USA where almost all psychoanalysts are medically qualified, there was no natural progression to analysis being offered on the NHS as it developed with the welfare state in 1948. This has led to practitioners traditionally working from rented consulting rooms or from a designated consulting room in their own home. As counselling and psychotherapy have grown out of psychoanalysis, their practitioners have followed a similar path in relation to their place of work where they have chosen to work in independent practice. (See Hudson-Allez Chapter 2 for more on the history of counselling.)

Advantages and disadvantages to working from home

Advantages

Perhaps the main advantage to working from home for the practitioner is the fact that they do not have to pay rent which can amount to as much as a third of their fee. Fees for rent are inevitably dependent on location with those in Brighton, for example, sometimes being as much as half of those in London, depending on the size and locality of the room required. There is also an obvious saving in travel expenses.

Working from home makes long-term work more viable as the room rental does not have to be passed on to the client in the therapist's fee. For the same reason another financial advantage is that it makes offering a sliding scale fee a more realistic option. Other advantages may be more practical than as a means of saving money. Without the financial constraints imposed by session times set by an organization letting rooms, working from home allows us the choice of working with longer gaps between clients if we prefer. It also offers flexibility as to when clients can attend. If a client has a job that takes them away from home so that they are unable to commit to attending therapy at the same time each week, working from home enables the therapist to offer alternative times. It also gives the therapist an opportunity to make use of the time doing something else should they want to if a client is unable to attend for some reason.

Finally, it allows the therapist free rein to furnish the room as they choose. Working in an agency or renting a room in a clinic may involve having to share that room with other therapists, perhaps with different kinds of therapists, who work at different times of the day and use the room and its furniture in a different way. Here the therapist has less control over the physical sur-roundings that may influence how comfortable they feel. This inevitably has an effect on how they function therapeutically. Choosing to work in a general clinic such as a natural health clinic, for example, may mean that the therapist is not able to work in a room that is a dedicated specifically to psychotherapy or counselling with appropriate furniture and soundproofing. I have worked in places where I have had to begin the day by rearranging furniture. This can be time consuming and irritating, especially if they are paying for this time and may lead to the counsellor feeling resentful. This in turn may affect how they relate to their clients. For example, one colleague of mine worked in a room where there was a massage table that she was not able to remove or collapse. This led to the client feeling anxious that the counsellor might be about to suggest that she give him a massage. Although much fantasy material was provided, she found that the anxiety it created was an unnecessary distraction.

Therefore working from home gives us far more control over our working environment. We also have the added bonus of not having to deal with the internal politics of another organization. In itself this can be distracting to the therapist and clients can inadvertently become caught up within it. For example, some clinics need to know if the therapist is not using the room on a particular day so that they can let it to another practitioner. This can lead to mistakes being made and rooms being double booked with the inevitable distressing consequences.

There have been occasions when I have seen some clients at home as well as in a hired consulting room, sometimes having one session per week in each venue if I have not had two free sessions available in one place. Although this is not an ideal situation I have been surprised by how easily clients have adapted to the two different environments. Some people have said that they prefer to see me at home as they feel that my home consulting room creates a more 'intimate' atmosphere. Others may find that added intimacy intimidating while others have said that they do not mind either room; the relationship with me with its clearly set boundaries being the most important thing that has maintained the 'therapeutic frame' (Langs 1977).

Having said this, inevitably there are likely to be many new issues to deal with. For example, if the therapist has seen a client at home to begin with they may be used to the anonymity of this. To then see the same therapist in a clinic where they wait in a public waiting room may be problematic for them. They may feel cheated or robbed of the intimacy experience by seeing them at home. That in turn may make the client feel that they are less important than the clients that they imagine the therapist still sees at home. Working the other way round (seeing the client in a clinic setting and then seeing them at home) may arouse anxieties about increased intimacy. The therapist is inviting them into their home that they may also share with their family. They may experience this as the therapist symbolically inviting them into their family, which Syme (2002) suggests is a therapy in itself. The client may have fantasies about other clients that they see at home and whether or not it is only 'special' clients that they see there. All these fantasies can provide material with which to work.

Disadvantages

One of the main disadvantages, indeed a potential danger of only working from home is the increased likelihood of the therapist becoming isolated from the rest of the world. The therapist is also in danger of living their life vicariously through their interesting clients. If the therapist is single and also lives alone this might be intensified. If they are also lonely and feeling vulnerable, they put themselves in a dangerous position if they work with clients who are feeling equally lonely. Clients are likely to intuit this and the likelihood of the therapist breaking boundaries and allowing him or herself to be seduced by a needy client is greater. Alternatively the therapist may become seductive him or herself. Syme (2002) notes the potential for unethical practice in the therapist who works in the isolation of their home and stresses the need not only for supervision to counter this, but also meeting with other independent colleagues or attending a local counselling association. This would offer the appropriate support that is necessary in this emotionally demanding work.

Depending on where we live, we may be excluding certain client groups. It may be prohibitively expensive, for example, to make adaptations to our home for wheelchair access. As I live in the countryside where there is no station nearby this excludes clients who do not drive.

Another disadvantage of working from home is the possible effect that it has on other family members. I will return to this later in more detail.

Accommodation

In ideal circumstances the counsellor or therapist who works from home should be able to provide a consulting room, a waiting room for clients who arrive early and a lavatory, all separate from the rest of the home. Syme (2002) suggests that a house that was previously owned by a GP, for example, would be ideal, although in reality this is rarely possible; salaries are insufficiently high to fund such facilities. Therefore it is most likely that a separate therapy room is made available. Ideally this should have a separate entrance from the rest of the house in order to protect the client's confidentiality and anonymity. This would also protect the therapist's family from feeling that they have to restrict movements and noise leading to the feeling that they come second to the therapist's clients. Again, this is often not possible to arrange due to financial implications.

Where it is not possible to have a completely separate therapy room, Syme (2002) also suggests that a room that doubles as a spare room for guests is an acceptable alternative, preferably with a sofabed rather than a single bed to act as couch for the client. A single bed is obviously inappropriate as it may give clients the impression that something sexual may be about to take place. If a single bed must be in the room, it is a good idea to disguise it with cushions and a rug. Similarly, if this room is upstairs we may need to be mindful of how the client experiences this. In a house we usually go upstairs to bed, indeed the room may be near to your bedroom. In order to protect our own privacy and so as not to embarrass the client with too much information about our personal life, it is a good idea to ensure that upstairs bedroom doors are kept closed. The implications of revisiting the primal scene are obvious.

In the home that I am in at the moment I am lucky enough to have a separate studio in the garden to the side of the main house that is only used for work. The situation of this building was an important factor in choosing the house. However, it is not perfect. There is no waiting room so I have to explain this to new clients and ask them to wait in their car if they arrive early. Neither is there a lavatory near to the room. The disadvantage is that if anyone does need to use the lavatory they have to go into the main house. As I work mostly in the evenings my children and the chaos of the mealtime are still very much in evidence. Having said this I am always surprised by how few people ask to use the facilities compared with when I lived in a flat where clients had to walk past the bathroom to reach the consulting room. I can only presume that they feel that because of the separateness of the house it feels more of an intrusion on my personal space. I regret that I am giving an implicit message that it is not acceptable for clients to need to go to the lavatory while they are with me. However, for me to suggest this in the therapy does feel rather awkward unless it is prompted by the clients themselves.

Some therapists agree to share a room with a colleague or partner who also works as a therapist. Here it is sensible to have some kind of agreement about the decor and layout of the room so that both parties feel comfortable working there. The decision as to whether or not to keep therapy books in the consulting room is also pertinent if two people are sharing the room. For example, I share a room with my husband who is a psychologist as well as a therapist and although the room does house our joint collection of psychotherapy books there are also his academic psychology books on the shelves. This offers the client an ambiguous message about who I might be.

Some people choose not to have any books in the therapy room believing that they distract and intimidate the client. Although this may sometimes be the case, the presence of the books can also be a way of 'focusing awe' (Frank 1975) in a positive sense, giving the message that the therapist is well read and knows what they are doing. Problems may arise if clients ask to borrow books, however. One client asked to borrow a book from my shelf because she believed that it might give her some answers to the dilemmas she was facing. Suddenly I was faced with a quandary. Should I lend her the book willingly or should I say no and risk her feeling rejected by me? I decided to explore her fantasies about how she believed that the book might help her. What finally emerged was the client's desire to take something of me away with her, a book that I had also touched and read that would give her the answers that I was seemingly withholding from her. She felt that the book might also give her more insight into me. Once we were able to explore and understand this, her need to take the book diminished. Had I allowed her to borrow the book, which was a very theoretical one, I think that she would have felt alienated and confused by its content, and ultimately frustrated that her questions were not answered.

Whether or not to lend books to clients is also a boundary issue and one that is perhaps more open to becoming blurred if we work from home. If we work psychodynamically, it is unlikely that we would lend a client a book as it would be colluding with the client's need to take more of us than is defined by the therapeutic hour. However, if the book and the client are in the same room, then this boundary may be more easily overlooked. Therapists working with different models such as cognitive behavioural therapy may feel that this is less important than lending the client something that might be of benefit to them.

Ultimately therefore, the main difference in the therapist working from home from the client's point of view is that it gives them more access to the therapist's personal life than if they worked from an impersonal rented consulting room. Depending on how personal or neutral the consulting room at home is kept, there is material to work with here. Very occasionally one of my children has left evidence of their existence by leaving a toy in the room that I have not noticed until after a client has arrived. This not only informs the client that I have children but it also has the potential to contaminate the safety of the therapeutic space. On one occasion a client had a fantasy that my children might have been playing in the room and that they may have been able to get into locked files and read my notes. Again depending on the model of working, these fantasies can be explored, so giving more understanding and meaning to the client's experience. Having said this I would still prefer not to have the toy in the room. There is usually plenty of material to explore that the client brings with them so any extras are not required. It is pertinent to say, however, that it does not have to be a disaster if something from outside the 'therapeutic frame' (Langs 1977) does find its way into the work, so long as it is kept to a minimum.

Dealing with envy

The potential for blurring the boundaries between our personal home life and our professional life can feel burdensome and unhelpful both in the therapeutic relationship and for us personally. Dealing with a client's envy of our perceived financial status (gleaned from the size of our house perhaps, or the value of property in our neighbourhood) is something that we may have to work with. However, it can feel wearisome to have to deal with a client's destructive envy (Klein 1957: 43–60), particularly if their fantasies mirror something that we also find difficult. Someone being envious of our perceived financial status, for example, can feel very demanding, especially if we are struggling financially ourselves at that time. Supervision is obviously an important source of support to the therapist here. Similarly, given the possibility that if we do have children then clients are likely to discover this at some point and they may feel envious of what they see as the ideal family. Working through these feelings with one of my clients enabled her to move from the nearby town in order to give her own children the experience of living in the countryside. It also meant that she was now able to work from home as she had more space. As discussed in Chapter 10 on endings where the therapist is pregnant, knowledge that we have children can often make clients feel envious of our children who appear to have more of our time and attention than the client does.

Equally, clients who are not in a relationship or who are struggling in an unhappy one may feel envious if they see our partner working in the garden or in the kitchen, potentially perceiving our relationship as the ideal partnership. Again these feelings are important to work with, offering a way into the client's emotional world; a gift that would otherwise be unavailable if we worked in an agency or rented consulting room.

It is also worth mentioning that if we are working from home we are party to information about the client that we would not necessarily gain if we work in a rented consulting room. For example, if a client parks their car outside our house or in our drive the close proximity gives us insight into the client's life that they do not necessarily consciously bring into the therapy room. How we feel about this may also colour the work. One supervisee, a married man with three teenage children, described to me how he had trouble resisting his urge to look over a client's expensive sportscar. He coveted it for himself. He realized that his envy of the client's financial status made it difficult for him to empathize with his distress about his girlfriend leaving him.

The effect on family life

Addressing the envy that our own family members may experience and act out, however, can be more challenging to manage successfully. Children may be envious of the time we spend with our clients. As Syme (1994) observes, children 'will be aware that the clients are being given uninterrupted time: something they may rarely get for themselves'. Indeed they have to share a part of their home with people who they cannot know (Syme 2002). My children have employed various techniques in letting me know how angry they feel about this, ranging from secretly spying on clients as they arrive to making extra noise at bedtime when I am working.

Although my own children have grown up knowing that I see clients at home some evenings in the week they always complain and often feign ignorance that this is the night that I work. When one of my daughters was about four years old she was very excited to tell me one morning that she had caught a glimpse of a client on their way out the evening before. She believed that she had seen something illicit. She knew implicitly that she was not meant to know anything about the client, but did not have the understanding as to why this confidentiality was important. I felt sad that she was trying to fathom out this material from the adult world at such a young age.

My husband and I have both tried to be sensitive to the fact that our working from home will have an effect on our children. In an attempt to minimize the negative impact, we try to work when they are at school or in childcare, during the evenings when they are on their way to bed with the parent who is not working, or when they are asleep. However, I think that the greatest impact is that we have to be conscious of how we talk about our work. For example, we need to make sure that we do not talk about work in ways that would breach clients' confidentiality, but in a way that does not make the children feel that our clients are more important than they are. I believe that this is where the potential harm may arise. Our work is surrounded by secrecy and yet it takes place at such close physical proximity to where our children are living so that they cannot but be affected by it.

In homes where the parents are not psychotherapists, their work may well be discussed over the supper table. The children may take little obvious notice, but the conversation will be part of their everyday experience and perception of their parents' lives. Fortunately for us, we both work in other organizations too so that our children do hear about other ordinary work dynamics, but where this is not the case trying to normalize not discussing work in front of the children is extremely challenging and possibly damaging for the children. Storr (1979) describes the potential impact of this eloquently and suggests a comparison between families of therapists with those of politicians and spies who are in possession of state secrets and who have to be careful about what they say:

> professional discretion means that the therapist is virtually unable to discuss his work with his family who often have very little idea of what his work entails. If either parent is a full-time, or even part time therapist, this means that the interchange within the family is diminished.
>
> (Storr 1979: 183)

While this is pertinent when working in any location, it is exacerbated when working from home. The confidentiality and the appearance to onlookers of our work being shrouded in secrecy are not only difficult for children to manage, but partners can also find it frustrating and alienating. I supervised a student who was having difficulties in his marital relationship. His wife was not a therapist and felt very threatened by him working late into the evening, often with women clients. She would accuse him of behaving inappropriately with them as a way of communicating her envy of his new profession and her anxiety that he was enjoying more intimate relationships with women other than with her. Understandably the therapist was very concerned by this and found it difficult to work while having fantasies that his wife might be listening at the door, not to mention how this might be affecting his clients.

Even when not experiencing overt relationship difficulties, the therapist's personal relationships may be more vulnerable to such anxieties when the work takes place under the same roof as the rest of the family. It is therefore important to make time to focus positively on the relationship and talk about the difficult feelings that arise. Perhaps more so than other professional parents, if we are not to overburden our children we need to think very seriously about how many hours of work we do. Barnett (2002: 113) recommends that: 'Sufficient quantity and quality time be spent together with each individual child, so that a close relationship is developed and maintained.' She suggests that children can then be enabled to weather the storms of periods of problematic family dynamics such as our emotional withdrawal from time to time.

I have certainly greatly decreased my hours with each successive child that I have had, not only because I have wanted to be at home with them during their first three years, but also because I have not had the emotional energy to be both a mother and full-time therapist. As Barnett (2002) points out: 'The emotional stress of therapy work can be long-lasting and extreme at times. This can drain the energies available for family life.'

Although this will change as the children grow older, having to work less has had an effect on my professional status. I have often been unable to attend conferences that involve staying away overnight and have been less available to accept teaching opportunities. The slowing down of my career journey is balanced, however, by the pleasures that my individual children bring. The personally enriching process of becoming a parent has also enhanced my skills and understanding that I am now able to bring to my work with clients.

For a therapist-parent working from home, there might be the mistaken view that they are still around and near their children while they are working. I have often found this to be a painful conflict; having to divide my loyalties between my children and my clients. Similarly, a colleague described how this is particularly difficult when one of the children was ill and wanted Mummy and not Daddy to put them to bed. She described having to divest herself of the pain on hearing her small child's screams of protest as she left him to receive the client. Even though she knew that her son would be fine once she had gone, the guilt was still unbearable. This sense of guilt may be intensified when the therapist is also feeling secretly relieved to be handing the responsibility over to another when they have been at home with the children all day. Inevitably clients may also hear what is going on and feel uncomfortable about taking the therapist away from her children. While this could create tension within the therapeutic relationship, it also has the potential to provide further material for the client and therapist to explore.

As mentioned above, Freud worked from home and his ideas emerged from within a complex domestic environment. While the Freud children were still young, Minna Bernays, Freud's sister-in-law, came to live with the family and shared the upbringing of the children with Martha, Freud's wife. Bernays became an intellectual confidante to Freud, playing a crucial role in the early years of his theoretical discoveries. Martha, on the other hand, showed little interest in her husband's work and preferred him to leave it locked away in the study along with his collection of antiquities. She described his work as 'pornography' but did acknowledge that there was also a 'kindness and a wisdom' there too (Freud Museum webpage 2005). Freud managed to work regardless of his wife's ambivalence and despite the presence of his six children in the flat below his consulting room in Vienna. Freud formulated his psychoanalytic technique on a basis of trial and error and acknowledges this by saying:

> The technical rules which I am putting forward have been arrived at from my own experience in the course of many years, after unfortunate results had led me to abandon other methods.
>
> (Freud 1912: 111)

Psychoanalysis, then, was born out of a family environment, so perhaps working from home with all its challenges may still be an appropriate place for the therapist or counsellor to work today. The therapist need not be afraid of experimenting with ways of balancing family life with working from home, providing that it is within an ethical framework.

Confidentiality

Just as information about our personal life is likely to filter into the therapeutic relationship when we work from home, it is important to be aware of the dangers of what goes on in that relationship being leaked out inappropriately into our home lives. It may be more tempting to breach confidentiality by coming into the kitchen after a difficult session to offload on to a partner. This is something that we might avoid by travelling home in the car and having time to think and process the session if we work from a rented consulting room. Alternatively, we might be able to discuss the case appropriately with a colleague if we work within an agency as a means of receiving immediate support. Similarly, as my husband is also a psychotherapist, I have often had to frustrate my desire to gain some instant supervision after a particularly painful or difficult session.

Where we keep our notes is important wherever we work. However, if we work from home the client is more aware that if not locked safely away his or her notes may be read by other family members. Therefore it is sensible to have a lockable filing cabinet in the consulting room in which to keep any notes. That way the client has physical evidence that you take care of confidentiality whether you spell this out to them from the beginning or not.

When we work from home our clients are also vulnerable to the gaze of neighbours who may be inquisitive about what we do. We may need to think about how much we tell them, but also consider the impact on them of clients turning up on an hourly basis. Extra cars parked in the street or in a shared driveway may well be frustrating for them. Friends who are visiting other family members in the house may need to get used to the idea that if one parent works from home its a good idea not to arrive between ten minutes to the hour and on the hour so as to avoid bumping into clients. Although some friends have been puzzled and slightly amused by this, they have soon become accustomed to it as one of our quirky 'rules'. Once again, these dynamics can also intrude on the therapeutic work which could be experienced as destructive or as an opportunity for further reflection.

Finally, in order to protect confidentiality a separate telephone line is useful. There is nothing worse for an anxious client to make the initial contact only to find the phone is answered not by the therapist themselves but by a relative or a child. Will they remember to give the message to the therapist? A separate line with an answerphone also protects our personal space. Particularly as I have small children who occasionally do have times when they scream and shout, to have a telephone call from a new client at these times would be extremely offputting for the client and for me. One disadvantage of an answerphone, however, is that some people do not like them or are unused to them. It is possible to have a message that conveys information about how you monitor your calls and about when you are available to have a direct conversation should the client not want you to call them.

With a separate telephone line we can also better protect ourselves from being drawn into doing telephone therapy on an ad hoc basis at inconvenient times. It is very difficult to tell a distressed client over the phone that you do not do telephone consultations. It is helpful to be clear at the contracting stage as to whether you are prepared to do telephone sessions and how much you charge for this. Personally I prefer to let clients know that if they feel the need to phone me between sessions then it would help them more to arrange an extra face to face session to help them over that particularly difficult phase.

Safety

Issues of safety are particularly relevant if we work from home. We may need to think about what kind of client group we see, perhaps refusing to work with people with a history of violent behaviour. Should we decide to see these people, then it is a good idea only to see them if we know that there is someone else on the premises who could help us should the need arise. At the very least we need to make sure that we have a clear escape route planned should the occasion arise. Syme (2002) suggests having a panic button installed, but this implies expense as well as the need for a clear set of procedures and another person to be available while we are working. It also puts the therapist on the defensive by its very existence, and will undoubtedly affect the therapeutic relationship.

Of course we do not always know the history of new clients before the initial assessment session. In this case it would be wise to make sure that there is somebody else on the premises for the initial assessment session. It may also help to make the client feel safer if they sense that there is somebody else around in the vicinity. If the therapist has concerns it might be an advisable idea to do the initial assessment in the safety of a clinic if he or she has the possibility of doing so. This offers the potential of deciding whether or not to see the client at home.

Insurance is also important and easily forgotten. However, both the BACP and UKCP insist on accredited members being insured.

It would be sensible to check whether or not professional indemnity insurance will insure against a client who slips on a slippery stone while on the therapist's premises, or whether they need separate public liability insurance (Syme 1994). Ordinary household insurance will not cover injury to a client unless the fact that the therapist's home is being used for business purposes has been specifically disclosed to the insurance company (Syme 2005).

Bond (2000) suggests that objections to counsellors and psychotherapists requiring insurance on the grounds that they are less at risk of harming a client than a doctor who works directly on the patient's body are unconvincing. This argument would certainly not support a psychotherapist who uses body work (Bioenergetics or Hakomi). The idea that insurance may encourage litigation by clients and defensive practice by counsellors and psychotherapists is also spurious. Any therapist working with the erotic transference would be seriously hampered were they overly concerned about client litigation. Bond emphasizes the counsellor's ethical responsibility to ensure that a client can be adequately compensated for should they have an accident while on their premises. He also points out that having adequate insurance also protects the professional; preparing a legal defence against a relatively minor claim can be extremely expensive.

Syme (2005) highlights the fact that ensuring a client does not suffer psychological harm is significantly more complex than ensuring their physical safety. If it is proven that a client has suffered psychological harm either through the counsellor's error, malpractice or omission, the claims are frequently high, as are the legal costs. Similarly, in the case of a client making a malicious claim against the therapist, the legal fees incurred by the therapist in simply defending against this are considerable. Therefore in an increasingly litigious society the need for insurance becomes essential whether working from home or not.

Finally, we need to consider that if we are using our home for business purposes we may be liable for a higher rate of council tax, depending on the number of hours we work.

Conclusion

My preferred way of working is combining working from home with working in a clinic where I rent a room in a nearby town. This gives me a sense of going out to work and therefore a feeling of professionalism that working solely from home does not always engender. Slipping away from the family and working at home may be convenient, but I do also enjoy the drive to the clinic as a transitional space in which to think and reflect upon my work.

The advantage of combining two working environments is that the therapist is able to meet up with colleagues. This addresses the dangers of working in isolation. It also gives the practitioner a potential referral source that can feed their practice at the clinic and at home.

Working from home introduces a wholly different set of dilemmas for the therapist to manage. At worst the issues that the family's presence raise can feel like a burden that we might prefer to avoid, but at best it adds a multifaceted dimension that enriches our thinking and experience which we then take to the work. We do not all have to be like Freud, but providing that we are able to manage adequately the challenges mentioned above, something precious emerges from our ability to survive the chaos of family life that allows us to experience a kind of humility with our clients. This is perhaps denied to us if we work in a neat and organized haven in a consulting room away from home.

References

Barnett, T. (2002) A therapist in the family, in J. Clark (ed.) *Freelance Counselling and Psychotherapy Competition and Collaboration*, Hove and New York: Brunner-Routledge.

Bond, T. (2000) *Standards and Ethics for Counselling in Action*, London: Sage.

Frank, J. (1975) *Persuasion and Healing: Comparative Study of Psychotherapy*, New York, NY: Schocken Books.

Frank, J. D. and Frank, J. B. (1993) *A Comparative Study of Psychotherapy*, 3rd edn, Baltimore, MA: Johns Hopkins University Press.

Freud, S. (1912) Recommendations to physicians practising psychoanalysis, in J. Strachey (ed. and trans.) *Standard Edition*, Vol. 12, London: Hogarth Press (1923).

Klein, M. (1957) *Envy and Gratitude*, London: Tavistock (pp. 43–60).

Langs, R. (1977) *The Therapeutic Interaction: A Synthesis*, New York: Jason Aronson.

Storr, A. (1979) *The Art of Psychotherapy*, London: Methuen.

Syme, G. (1994) *Counselling in Independent Practice*, Maidenhead: Open University Press.

—— (2002) Working from home: a psychotherapist with long-term clients, in J. Clark (ed.) *Freelance Counselling and Psychotherapy: Competition and Collaboration*, Hove and New York: Brunner-Routledge.

—— (2005) Private practice, insurance, advertising, in C. Felthan and I. Horton (eds) *The Sage Handbook of Counselling and Psychotherapy*, London: Sage.

Website

Freud Museum: www.freud.org.uk

Chapter 9

The role of money in the therapeutic exchange

Rosalind Field and Adrian Hemmings

He that wants money, means, and content is without three good friends.

(Shakespeare, *As You Like It*, act 3, sc. 2, 24–26)

Introduction

The exchange of money for services between client and therapist is one of the defining differences in working in independent practice and working within an organization where their employer pays the counsellor a salary. The way in which we relate to money affects us in so many different areas of our lives; perhaps because of this money is represented in most of Maslow's hierarchy of needs (Maslow 1970). Inevitably the way in which the client and the therapist relate to money will be played out in the therapeutic relationship and as such can either impede the work or provide a valuable area to explore. It has been the focus of discussion for many years (Allen 1971; Forester 1997; Valentine 1999).

In this chapter we begin by offering a definition of money from differing perspectives and then go on to relate that to clinical counselling. We explore the themes that might be present in the way in which the client relates to money and how this may be mirrored in their relationship with themselves. What is the client's attitude to money and how do they manage it? Who pays for the sessions? How might the client's relationship with money be played out in the relationship with the therapist?

The therapist will also have their own way of relating to money and this will impact on how they work. It will affect their decision on which model to use, their formulation of their client's difficulties and how long they feel it is necessary to work with the client. The very nature of the physical environment in which the therapist works will also be an expression of this relationship. These two 'systems' come together in the therapeutic relationship and produce a wealth of potential ways of working with the client, an opportunity lost in other contexts. We conclude by discussing the context created by the fact that in independent practice the client is usually required to pay the therapist a fee and how this may differ from other contexts. First let us look at some general issues.

What is money?

We generally accept that money is a token of exchange. We receive it in exchange for our work and spend it in exchange for goods and services. As such, money can also be seen as a token energy source; we earn it in order to buy essentials such as food and clothing, heating and lighting and we may also use it to buy luxuries. When we part with our money we are hopefully gaining something for ourselves that will either help to sustain our existence or will make us feel more positive about ourselves. The nurture that we receive from this process enables us to earn more money. And so the cycle continues.

Those who are not part of this exchange process may inadvertently enter into an infantilized relationship with the world and their lack of financial resources is likely to sap personal energy. It is therefore unlikely that these people will seek a counsellor or psychotherapist working in independent practice. It is unfortunate that in the UK psychological treatment is divided between the little offered on the NHS and a few voluntary bodies who do often ask clients to pay a contribution to their therapy, and the other extreme of private provision which may be experienced as expensive and unattainable. NHS patients often have to wait over a year for treatment, by which time their symptoms or reasons for seeking therapy in the first place may have changed (personal communication). Therefore with the option of going to a private or independent therapist clients who can afford to 'can pay not to wait', leaving those who cannot afford it 'waiting not to pay'. This is the way that one local GP described the dilemma of private versus NHS treatment.

Money as a form of power

By coming to see a counsellor in independent practice the client is exercising his or her economic power. They are making a choice that someone with less financial resources may not be able to make (Buck 1999). A possible advantage of the client paying the therapist directly in an independent practice set-up is that the power imbalance between 'sick patient' and well 'expert' therapist is, in part, balanced out. They are buying a service and in many ways they are employing the therapist. In order to earn the money to pay for the therapy the client has to possess sufficient ego strength to enable them to function in the world with a degree of success.

Similarly the financial exchange with the therapist is also a reminder of the five levels of relationship postulated by Clarkson (2003); here the adult-to-adult contract that is made between therapist and client. This becomes very important if working with the transference where the client may project infantile feelings towards a parent on to the therapist and the therapist actively works with these projections. The ability to pay the therapist at the end of the session or at the end of the month serves as a reminder that these feelings are just that; they are an expression of a younger part of them and that they are not so regressed that they are unable to leave the therapy room and enter into their adult world. This is also pertinent when using any other therapeutic methods where the client becomes regressed as an important part of the process. It is questionable as to how offering free counselling and therapy is able to attend to this aspect of the work. Jung acknowledged that money would have helped him maintain the professional boundary between him and Sabina Spielrein, his patient with whom he had an affair (Carotenuto 1984).

Cultural implications of money

Different cultural groups relate to money in different ways. There is a stereotypical British reticence about discussing income or money in general. Indeed Temperley (1984) suggests that 'modern prudery is about money'. One of the strongest taboos is asking the price of something that someone has bought or worse still leaving the price tag on a gift that we have given to someone. This contrasts with the other stereotypes of being obsessed with money and

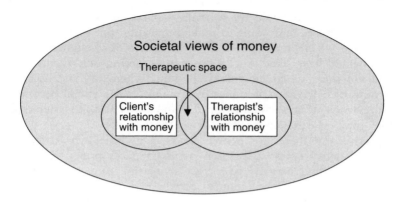

Figure 9.1 How societal views of money influence the therapeutic relationship

constantly talking about the price of things. Therefore, depending on the cultural background of the therapist and the client, discussing the therapist's fee may be difficult for both (Birnbach 1999). Figure 9.1 shows how societal views of money influence the therapeutic relationship.

How the client relates to money

The way in which we relate to money can be seen as a reflection of how we relate to ourselves. For example, do we spend money freely on others but have more difficulty spending on ourselves, or vice versa. If we constantly spend money on others and not on ourselves we may want to demonstrate our love for the other person, as we believe that is the only way we can communicate this feeling.

Some people feel the need to spend excessive amounts of money on their children, partners or spouses as a means of compensation for not giving them enough emotional attention. Therefore spending money becomes an expression of guilt. Eventually loved ones will see through this inauthentic transaction and retaliate in some way, possibly by expressing anger. This will have an inevitable effect on how the spender feels about himself or herself and consequently about those on whom they have spent money. It is possible that they will feel hurt and resentful that their love is being rejected, but will try to make reparation by repeating the process. Others may want to make reparation for what they did not have when they were children by giving their children what they would have liked, but in this process seeing only themselves and not their actual individual children. When this unconscious pattern of behaviour continues to fail and the individual becomes more aware of how unhappy or unfulfilled they feel, it is then that they may resort to counselling or psychotherapy.

Conversely there are people who have difficulties spending money and who portray themselves as having less money than they really have and may try to attract sympathy from others. They may need to hoard their money secretly as a means of protecting their vulnerability and against possible future catastrophe.

Other people spend more than they earn and are constantly borrowing money. This behaviour may be a reflection of a need, possibly originating in emotional needs not being satisfied during childhood. Alternatively, it may be interpreted as a refusal to take adult responsibility for themselves and a request that another looks after them. This may have a variety of origins.

Invariably the way in which people relate to money directly correlates with their sense of self-worth. Therefore, when a client's mode of relating to money is borne out of a sense of unworthiness it will have an inevitable impact on how they then relate to paying for their own therapy. For example, if a client has low self-worth they may opt to work with a trainee, paying a lower fee than for a fully experienced therapist even if they can afford the full fee. They do not feel entitled to the apparent advantages of experience. Research, however, suggests that trainee and recently qualified therapists achieve similar outcomes with clients with mild to moderate difficulties (Berman and Norton 1985).

John, a professional actor, came to see me when I was in training. Although he was successful in his work and currently working and relatively well paid, his image of himself was that he was not successful. In the past he had had several years 'resting' and had become depressed. Now that he was in work he felt able to attend to his low mood, but was concerned about the cost of the therapy. As the work progressed he began to arrive late to sessions. I suggested that his lateness might be an expression of his anger towards me. Further exploration revealed John's ambivalence about working with a therapist who was not 'fully qualified'. As the son of two 'successful' television actors John had been looked after by a series of young nannies. Consequently his mother became the elusive but much desired object of his affection. In choosing to work with a trainee (I was also in my mid-twenties) John had re-created the familiar scenario of his childhood and was secretly yearning for the real mother/qualified therapist who was going to fulfil all of his needs. This example highlights the usefulness of the therapist making their professional status clear to the client from the outset (BACP 2002).

Of course these are only a few examples and there are many more possibilities of how people relate to money. We may even recognize some of these modes of relating in ourselves. Although a prospective client is unlikely to be coming to therapy with these specific difficulties in mind, their relationship with money will reveal much about them. Inevitably their manner of relating to money will impact on the therapeutic relationship. When a client buys therapy as a service, do they see it as an essential or as a luxury? For some, therapy is perceived as a form of personal development, whereas for others it is a necessity created out of their despair. One client who came to see me believed that her coming to therapy was a matter of life or death. If she did not come she felt that her pain would become physical and would inevitably lead to her premature death. She was determined not to allow this to happen.

Others may be seeking counselling because they feel they have exhausted all other avenues and this is a last resort. They may have tried other forms of free counselling – often short-term counselling on the NHS or some low cost usually time-limited therapy provided by a voluntary organization, often administered by trainee or neophyte therapists. Therefore now paying for this service may be an enormous investment for them.

The therapist's relationship with money

While much of what has already been described can also be applied to the counsellor, there are issues that need to be examined which are specifically relevant to counsellors and how their relationship to money may impact on the therapeutic work. Are there any overall features of counsellors that may give us an insight into this? There have been several studies that have explored the characteristics of people who are attracted to the profession of counselling and psychotherapy (Kniveton 2004). One of the themes that has arisen from these studies is that of background and early childhood experience. It has been shown that many therapists are attracted to the profession as a way of addressing a reparative phantasy due to early experiences of caregiving and receiving (DiCaccavo 2002). By becoming therapists we fulfil a need to change the lives of others and so help heal our own psychic wounds. While this is certainly not true of all therapists, it is likely that the role of therapist is in itself fulfilling an important function for the practitioner and so being paid may be a secondary activity. Coming from this background may also have a profound effect on self-esteem, which as we have explored above is itself related to money. The gender of the therapist is also an important factor and societal views of how men and women should view payment are discussed by several authors (Gresham and Fontenot 1989; Lansky 1999; Motherwell 2002).

While these issues should be addressed during training and where appropriate the training therapy of practitioners, it may already set up a dynamic before the therapist has started working. Such issues as how much they should charge for their services and whether they should charge every client the same may also be affected by this dynamic. An interesting feature of the counselling profession is the number of counsellors who offer their service for free. How many other helping professionals offer free or very low cost therapy? The NHS has a large number of volunteer counsellors working in primary care and contracted voluntary organizations (McLeod 2000). Yet the number of doctors, nurses or social workers who are unpaid or who offer a free or nearly free service must be almost negligible. Quite why this phenomenon is so prevalent is yet to be fully explored and may well be a product of a body of practitioners whose roots are in the voluntary sector and who are developing their professional identity. Again one is left with the question as to why this is taking so long and what might be at the core of this practice? Is this related to practitioners' sense of value of themselves and their practice?

This brings us to another characteristic of the therapist that could impact on the exchange of money which is the therapist's belief in the efficacy of what they are offering. Someone who has a certainty that what they offer is of value is more likely to be at ease charging for it than someone who does not. This has two aspects: the therapy itself and worth of the therapist who is offering it. For example, many medical doctors have a profound belief that what they are offering is lifesaving and of considerable worth.

A view also held by most people in society is that many medical interventions are backed up by research, although this is actually much less than is imagined (Gill *et al.* 1996). Hence medical interventions become a valuable commodity and the people who offer them are valued and held in high esteem. In medicine there is also a clear distinction between practitioner and the intervention itself which can be quite separate such as when a pharmacological therapy is offered. Not so with clinical counselling. The counsellor and the intervention are inextricably linked and even in manualized therapies such as CBT it is the relationship that is consistently most associated with outcome (Bowers and Clum 1988).

Many counsellors have a poor understanding of research and so may have a vague understanding of why what they do is useful. It is recognized that not knowing (Casement 2002) is an important and sometimes uncomfortable aspect of clinical counselling and it is just this that may make us wonder if what we offer is worth what we charge. It is also important to recognize that a counsellor who is absolutely 'certain' is one to be avoided as they may fall into the Procrustean trap of attempting to fit their client into their theory instead of listening. O'Hanlon and Bertolino (1998) refer to this as 'theoretical countertransference'.

How might this relationship be communicated to clients? As mentioned in Chapter 8, the independent practitioner is in a unique situation in that many counsellors practise from home where clients have ample opportunity to scrutinize the house, the consulting room and even the car of the counsellor. All of which will provide food for fantasy about the therapist and their relationship with money.

The role that money plays in the therapeutic contract

Alongside confidentiality, frequency of attending, time boundaries and ground rules on behaviour, an agreement on how the exchange of money is managed is fundamental to the initial contract; again differentiating independent practice from other forms of counselling. How much should the counsellor charge, when should they be paid and what will happen when the client does not attend are all aspects of this negotiation. It is at this point that the counsellor's and client's relational styles with money first come into contact with each other.

How much the counsellor should charge will depend on a number of factors such as the local 'going rate', the level of experience of the counsellor, their political and philosophical beliefs which may be linked to their own sense of worth. There are also factors that the client brings such as their ability to pay, their employment status and whether they are paying for themselves.

Offering a sliding scale fee

In order to try to address the imbalance between waiting for an NHS therapist and having to pay for private therapy some therapists and counsellors offer a sliding scale fee. They set a minimum fee that they are prepared to accept and invite clients to place themselves on that scale, trusting that those who earn a higher salary are honest enough to pitch themselves at the higher end. Therefore the higher earners support the lower waged – a democratic ideal. However, in order to do this successfully without undermining one's own ability to earn enough to live on it is necessary to have a large practice, so that there is a balance of higher earners to low-waged clients, as it would be no good if all clients paid the lowest fee on the scale. Similarly it is important not to forget that 'the apparent largesse in waiving a fee can be both patronizing and an abuse of power' (Syme 1994).

However, the client's relationship with money does become more overt if we offer a sliding scale fee. Some clients may feel that they should pay the highest fee even if they cannot afford it, believing that in doing so they are getting the best service or because they are afraid of being seen by the therapist as being mean. Others will offer to pay the lower fee on the scale perhaps because they have a low sense of self-worth even though they may actually be able to afford to pay more. A new client arrived outside my room driving a new car and wearing expensive clothes. My immediate assumption was that he would have no problem paying the full fee, indeed he expected to do so himself. However, further exploration of his circumstances revealed that his business was on the brink of bankruptcy and as a result he was feeling overwhelmed and depressed. I felt that he would benefit from therapy and encouraged him to take up my offer of seeing him at a reduced fee until his circumstances changed. Although he found this difficult to accept as it meant acknowledging his vulnerability, something with which he was unfamiliar as a previously successful businessman, he benefited from the work that followed. Conversely, I had another client who dressed scruffily and drove an old car. She had a successful international business but was concerned with how other people would perceive her. While she enjoyed the idea that she could confound the expectations of her competitors and used this strategically to gain power over them, it also meant that she was unable to enjoy her success in a material way, which she began to realize she would like to do.

Here we can see the advantages and disadvantages of offering a sliding scale fee. The advantage is that by discussing where the clients place themselves on the sliding scale it offers the opportunity to explore the client's relationship with money and therefore an important aspect of themselves. The risk is that, initially at least, the client may misrepresent their circumstances at either their own or the therapist's expense by paying too much or too little and be resistant to exploring the issue further. Here we also see that our initial assumptions about clients may not always be accurate. It is therefore important and helpful to notice how both our assumptions and those of our clients are communicated, consciously or unconsciously.

The negotiation around the fee can have other difficult consequences. At the beginning of my work as a psychotherapist, a young woman student came to see me who had difficulty in paying any fee. A way of dealing with this appeared in the form of an area Local Economy Trading Scheme (LETS) scheme. There are many LETS schemes around the country and they have arisen as a way for unwaged people to have access to services that they could otherwise not afford. The system works on one person offering a service such as decorating or gardening and receiving a certain number of LETS tokens which can then be exchanged for other services such as music tuition, massage and counselling. In my attempt to make counselling more available to unwaged people, I agreed with my client that she could 'pay' me in LETS until she found a way of paying me in pounds. I charged my normal pound rate in LETS and we continued our work together. The LETS scheme encourages a certain level of debt with its members and after six months we reviewed our work together and her progress in finding other ways of paying me. It became apparent that not only had she not explored other ways of paying me but she had also done very little in terms of earning LETS. To add to this I was rapidly becoming very 'rich' in LETS but when I came to 'spend' them found that services I valued such as plumbing and brick-laying were grossly oversubscribed and consequently unavailable. Should I need my dog walked on an astral plane I would have had plenty to choose from, but as we were renovating our house at the time and didn't have a dog, this service was not immediately useful. To compound the issue further, I had a newsletter from the LETS scheme informing me that the Inland Revenue were investigating the scheme and were considering taxing LETS pound for LET at the standard rate. I was apparently about to pay my client to give her therapy. As can be imagined, this had an effect on the therapeutic relationship that needed to be addressed immediately. She left shortly after we agreed a fee in pounds.

This demonstrates a number of issues in the exchange of money. My haste to provide a politically acceptable solution was fuelled in part by guilt and the value that I placed on the service that I was offering. This 'relational style' was confronted with her views on money. How much should she spend on herself, her anger at the 'state' for not giving her her 'due' and the fact that her 'relational style' fitted very well with the LETS scheme. The result was that these issues could not be addressed in the therapy as we were both apparently getting what we wanted. It ended up with both of us arriving in a familiar position. Several years after this episode I was still left with almost a thousand LETS to remind me of this lesson and I still had no dog.

As Syme (2003) suggests, there are other complications in accepting barter and gifts in lieu of payment for therapy. She introduces the notion of a 'dual relationship' that is created between therapist and client. If the client provides a weekly pie or cake (her example), the therapist becomes the employer of the client and thereby the boundary issues become complicated. For example, potential issues arise if the therapist becomes bored with the cake or pie or if they are not up to standard. This may lead to the therapist feeling resentful of the client and therefore more at risk of acting out these feelings which would inevitably be abusive to the client. Similarly, how does one establish the value of one session of therapy with any other service being offered by the client? This was apparently already established with the LETS scheme, but still difficulties arose.

Another example comes from a very different relational style. In this case my client was a successful barrister with no difficulty in earning sufficient money. After working together for several months she told me that I did not charge her enough and that she thought that I ought to double my fees. While initially being seduced into feeling flattered by the value placed on our work and excited by the prospect of an imminent pay rise, I declined the offer and we took time to examine what this might mean in how she related to others. In her relationship with her partner she tended to be subservient except in the provision of money. She very much held the purse strings and managed money within the relationship to the extent that her partner didn't even have her own chequebook. This event gave us the opportunity to reflect on this and so enable her to become more assertive in other areas of her relationship. We were able to examine how she had attempted to exert fiscal power over me in order to redress the perceived power imbalance in our relationship.

Emotional prostitution

When the client pays the therapist directly for their therapy the notion of 'emotional prostitution' sometimes becomes apparent (Smail 2005). The client may feel that they are paying the therapist for an emotional service that they are unable to find elsewhere. This often generates anger in the client that leads them to despise the therapist and indeed themselves. I have sometimes had clients say to me that they think that the only reason that I am not being judgemental of them is because they are paying me to be 'nice' to them. They are unable to trust that I am not there to judge and misinterpret my non-judgemental response to what they have said or done as the kind of cut-off response that a prostitute may have to learn in order to do the work they do.

There may also be occasions when the therapist may have a countertransference response to a client where they feel that the client is treating them as though they are a prostitute. An extreme example of this is when a male client had great difficulty in acknowledging his anger towards me for not being able to give him 'enough'. One day he paid me in cash that included £20 in pound coins which he had to count out into my hands. In the following session I brought up the subject about how he had paid me in the previous session and we were able to explore his ambivalent feelings towards me. Eventually he was able to see that paying me the coins was a way of expressing his rage by trying to humiliate me while at the same time gaining a little more time with me as he counted out the money.

When a third party pays the fee

The issues around balancing the power relationship between therapist and client are mentioned above. However, they are only pertinent when the client is paying for the therapy himself or herself. They become more problematic when somebody else is paying (for more on the influence of the significant other see Adrian Hemmings' Chapter 5). For example, I had a client, a young man in his mid-twenties, whose mother was paying for his therapy. Cummings and Sayama's (1995) notion of the 'implicit and explicit contract' is helpful in understanding the communication he was imparting to me. The explicit contract that he made (which was conscious) was that he was here to work on his anger management, but the implicit (unconscious) contract was that he was here only because his mother wanted him to come as he was causing trouble in the family by getting into fights with his brother. He did not stay for very long, choosing to leave before the agreed time because he decided that he did not need therapy after all, so punishing his mother further, but perhaps exercising a newly discovered degree of autonomy.

Similarly if a spouse is paying, possibly even signing the cheques, the process may be reinforcing a sense of infantalization for the client. In systemic terms the person paying is also identifying the problem in the presenting patient/client (Minuchin and Fishman 1981) and therefore giving us information about the relationship between the couple. A depressed woman came to see me for therapy. Her husband paid for this and in so doing was able to absolve himself from any responsibility in her difficulties, projecting the problems in their relationship on to his wife. It was as though he felt he was doing something to help, but was really throwing money at the problem and not accepting his part. It later became apparent that my client's response of depression and 'sickness' was her way of expressing aggression towards her husband in a passive way – she was being depressed at him. Again the exploration of the client/couple's relationship and their relationship with money and how that affects their relationship with themselves and others becomes a useful opportunity that is unavailable in other work contexts.

Health insurance and employment assistance programmes

Different issues may arise if an insurance company or workplace pays for the therapy. Depending on the circumstances, the way in which the client relates to the organization paying for the therapy will have an effect on how they then use the therapy and how they relate to the therapist. Syme (1994) suggests that a client unconsciously may want to punish an employer by refusing to terminate the counselling and that the counsellor needs to be mindful not to collude with this. In fact many EAPs will now only offer to pay for a fixed number of sessions (between 5 and 12 typically). Therefore the likelihood of this happening is minimized. One client I worked with only really began to work productively within the therapeutic process once he had finished the course of therapy that his insurance company had agreed to pay for. It was as if he could not accept ownership of the space until he was actually paying for the service himself. It transpired that as a child he had always been expected to stand on his own two feet and be independent. He had been sent to boarding school from the age of seven and although he was very 'successful' in his work this disguised a vulnerability that he would not allow anybody to reach. Consequently he had difficulties with intimate relationships. It is debatable as to whether it was an issue of time, or whether it was fulfilling his need to be in control of paying that allowed this to be addressed. By feeling more trusting of me and contained by the extension of the therapeutic relationship the work moved on and we were able to explore both possibilities.

Of course it does not mean that unless the client pays for their own therapy there will be problems. If this were the case then therapy offered by the NHS and voluntary organizations would be ineffective and we know this not to be so. It is necessary to highlight that the process of the direct payment to the therapist does offer a valuable dynamic with which to work therapeutically.

Envy

Power and envy are inextricably linked (Klein 1957). An aspect of money is that it also has the potential to create envy that in turn can be destructive if it is not addressed. A client may be envious of the perceived income of the therapist. They may gain information about this from the physical environment in which we work – whether it is in our home (and which part of the neighbourhood this is) or if the consulting room is in a prestigious looking clinic. If we work from home the client may notice what make of car we drive and even though they may make false assumptions these will have an effect on how they perceive us and may make them feel envious. Again this is material that can be worked with. Perhaps more problematic is when we as therapists feel envious of our client's car and our perception of their income. During times when I have been working a minimum number of hours per week when my children were small I have sometimes felt envious of my clients having the time and financial resources to have something as luxurious as therapy – time to spend on themselves. I have also found myself feeling envious of well-dressed women clients, particularly when I have been in the later stages of pregnancy and not feeling particularly attractive myself. These are times when supervision has proved invaluable not only in containing my own feelings but also in exploring the meaning in terms of the client's process and their communication with me.

How the fee is paid

The way in which the client finally pays the therapist also informs us of how they perceive the relationship whether unconsciously or not. A client who always pays in cash may want to keep the relationship more confidential by not having any record on their bank account. However, they may also feel that they are doing the therapist a favour and imagine that the therapist will not declare the cash to the tax inspector. This fantasy may also give the client an increased sense of intimacy with the therapist, a feeling of collusion against the state.

If either the client or we ourselves request payment in advance, whether by cheque or cash, this is a way of ensuring that we do receive payment. However, there is also a danger that we inadvertently become the client's bank manager; we take the money before they have the opportunity to spend it on something else. Conversely, if the client pays at the end of the month we may risk not being paid at all if the client leaves before that time. However, by invoicing the client at the end of the month we do imply that we trust that the client will pay us. This thereby reinforces the contract made between two adults. Similarly a pay as you go

(Bond *et al.* 2005) system ensures a clarity about the payment and again serves as a reminder of the adult-to-adult transaction. This method of payment also attempts to balance the power dynamic between therapist and client. Inevitably there are cultural differences to take into consideration here; a client receiving state benefits or on a low wage is unlikely to be able to pay for more than one session at a time.

Conclusion

Many of the above issues do enter the therapeutic work in different guises and in other working contexts. However, it is through the conduit of payment for the service in independent practice that money takes on a greater meaning. It adds a powerful dynamic with which to work, offering the client another means to communicate with the therapist and for the therapist to understand the client. If the therapist is reflective and learns to feel comfortable speaking this extra tier of language, then what has the potential to be destructive within the relationship can be used creatively to the client's benefit.

References

Allen, A. (1971) The fee as a therapeutic tool, *Psychoanalysis Quarterly* 44: 132–140.

Berman, J. and Norton, N. (1985) Does professional training make a therapist more effective?, *Psychological Bulletin* 98: 401–407.

Birnbach, L. (1999) Funny money: the therapeutic fee and the patient's and analyst's relationship to money, *Issues in Psychoanalytic Psychology* 21(1 and 2): 21–31.

Bond, T., Alred, G. and Hughes, P. (2005) Clinical practice issues, in C. Feltham and I. Horton (eds) *The Sage Handbook of Counselling and Psychotherapy*, 2nd edn, London: Sage.

Bowers, T. G. and Clum, G. A. (1988) Relative contribution of specific and nonspecific treatment effects: meta-analysis of placebo-controlled behavior therapy research, *Psychological Bulletin* 103: 315–323.

British Association of Counselling and Psychotherapy (2002) *BACP Ethical Guidelines*, Rugby: BACP.

Buck, S. (1999) The function of the frame and the role of fee in the therapeutic situation, *Women-and-Therapy* 22: 37–50.

Carotenuto, A. (1984) A secret symmetry: Sabina Spielrein in between Jung and Freud, New York: Pantheon.

Casement, P. (2002) *Learning From Our Mistakes: Beyond Dogma in Psychoanalysis and Psychotherapy*, New York: Guilford Press.

Clarkson, P. (2003) *The Therapeutic Relationship*, 2nd edn, London: Whurr.

Cummings, N. A. and Sayama, M. (1995) *Focused Psychotherapy: A Casebook of Brief, Intermittent Psychotherapy throughout the Life Cycle*, Philadelphia: Taylor/Francis.

DiCaccavo, A. (2002) Investigating individuals' motivations to become counselling psychologists: the influence of early caretaking roles within the family, *Psychology and Psychotherapy: Theory, Research-and-Practice*, 75(4): 463–472.

Forester, J. (1997) *Truth Games: Lies, Money and Psychoanalysis*, Cambridge, MA: Harvard University Press.

Gill, P., Dowell, A. C., Neal, R. D., Smith, N., Heywood, P. and Wilson, A. E. (1996) Evidence based general practice: a retrospective study of interventions in one training practice, *British Medical Journal* 312: 819–821.

Gresham, A. and Fontenot, G. (1989) The different attitudes of the sexes toward money: an application of the money attitude scale, *Advances in Marketing* 8: 380–384.

Klein, M. (1957) *Envy and Gratitude*, New York: Basic Books.

Kniveton, B. H. (2004) Influences and motivations on which students base their choice of career, *Research in Education* 72: 47–57.

Lansky, E. (1999) Psychotherapist's ambivalence about fees: male and female differences, *Women and Therapy* 22: 5–23.

McLeod, J. (2000) The importance of the voluntary sector in the provision of counselling services, talk delivered at the Annual General Meeting of the Dundee branch of Couple Counselling, Scotland, 7 June.

Maslow, A. H. (1970) *Motivation and Personality*, 2nd edn, New York: Harper and Row.

Minuchin, S. and Fishman, H. C. (1981) *Family Therapy Techniques*, Cambridge, MA: Harvard University Press.

Motherwell, L. (2002) Women, money, and psychodynamic group psychotherapy, *International Journal of Group Psychotherapy* 52(1): 49–66.

O'Hanlon, B. and Bertolino, B. (1998) *Even from a broken web. Brief respectful solution oriented therapy for sexual abuse and trauma*, New York: Wiley.

Smail, D. (2005) *Power, Interest and Psychology Elements of a Social Materialist Understanding of Distress*, Ross-on-Wye: PCCS Books.

Syme, G. (1994) *Counselling in Independent Practice*, Maidenhead: Open University Press.

Syme, G. (2003) *Dual Relationships in Counselling and Psychotherapy: Exploring the Limits (Ethics in Practice)*, England: Sage.

Temperley, J. (1984) Settings for psychotherapy, *British Journal of Psychotherapy* 1: 101–112.

Valentine, L. M. (1999) The case nexus: or how the therapeutic fee is a form of communication, *British Journal of Psychotherapy* 15: 334–346.

Chapter 10

Breaks and endings in independent practice

Rosalind Field

And whether we shall meet again I know not.
Therefore our everlasting farewell take;
For ever and for ever farewell. Cassius!
If we do meet again, why, we shall smile;
If not, why then this parting was well made.

O, that a man might know
The end of this day's business ere it come!
But it sufficeth that the day will end,
And then the end is known.
(Shakespeare, *Julius Caesar*, Brutus to Cassius,
act 5, sc. 1, 122–125)

Introduction

All relationships come to an end, whether through the death of one party or by agreement (or not) between the two parties. Similarly, therapeutic relationships come to an end and there is much in the literature on the nature and significance of the ending process (Mann 1973). I begin this chapter with a broad discussion on the meaning of saying goodbye in relationships in general and move on to relate this to the therapeutic relationship in independent practice. I will go on to explore the issues raised by different kinds of ending: unplanned endings caused by illness of either the client or therapist; interprocess endings created by client or therapist taking holidays; and planned endings including endings of individual sessions. I explore breaks and endings simultaneously as the clinical issues that they raise, such as separation anxiety (Bowlby 1978) and loss of an object (Winnicott 1971) are very similar.

Underlying any therapeutic ending is the emotional management of loss for the client. The therapist also experiences loss. It may well be an emotional loss felt for that particular client which is largely due to the composite attachment styles of the client and therapist (Marris 1974; Bowlby 1978; Parkes 2004). There is also the loss of the therapist's income. By the nature of self-employment the independent practitioner is financially more vulnerable than their employed colleagues. Therefore in the section on fiscal dependence I explore the vulnerability of the counsellor in independent practice where the client decides to end the process prematurely, before the agreed time and without discussion with the counsellor. I explore what this may mean for the client and the practitioner.

Although this book presupposes that the therapist will have undergone a substantial period of personal therapy during their training, inevitably issues will arise once the therapist begins to practise independently that may take them by surprise; these may be either personal or professional issues. Indeed some issues around endings may only be faced when the therapist has their own personal crisis such as prolonged illness or pregnancy. Using examples from my own experience, I discuss some of the professional issues that may arise in these situations. I pay particular attention to issues raised when the therapist becomes pregnant because as yet there is little in the literature that explores this.

If the ending feels unplanned or messy, the therapist may feel a loss of professional autonomy and a temporary loss in confidence. Without the support of colleagues the therapist who works independently may experience these feelings more acutely (see Adrian Hemmings on collegial support, Chapter 5).

In this chapter I discuss the context of the referral to the independent practitioner, the way in which the therapeutic contract is made, including how the ending is decided. I explore the issues raised by different kinds of ending: unplanned endings caused by illness of either the client or therapist; interprocess endings created by client or therapist taking holidays; and planned endings, including endings of individual sessions.

Finally I explore the feelings of loss experienced by the client when the therapist moves house or consulting room. I also briefly discuss the subject of the counsellor having a long-term illness and the controversial idea of making preparations for the therapist's unexpected death.

Although I take a predominantly psychodynamic approach, the issues raised are pertinent to most therapeutic styles adopted in independent practice. I use the words 'counsellor' and 'therapist' interdependently.

Saying goodbye

Saying goodbye marks a severance of contact with another person, punctuating one experience so that we can move on to the next. We have developed a ritual process that helps to contain the feelings that surround the experience of breaking the contact with the other. At one end of the emotional spectrum such as in formal or business relationships, we shake hands before we part. Where there is a deeper emotional connection between family member or friends, for example, we may kiss one another goodbye. Here the goodbye process helps us to hold the other in mind throughout the separation period until we meet again.

In the quotation at the beginning of this chapter, Brutus is contemplating the ultimate form of ending, death before a battle, and wants to say his last farewell to Cassius. Although death is the definitive farewell, depending on the degree of emotional connection between the parties an ordinary goodbye can feel like a small death. It is an ending and it is sometimes painful, yet when it is avoided we may feel that we have missed out on something important. We need only to look to the morning playground where a small child has suddenly noticed that his mother has gone – he was too busy playing when she kissed him goodbye. Now he believes that she went without saying the all-important words and he is distraught.

Reassuring phrases such as 'See you soon', 'Au revoir' and the children's rhyme, 'See you later alligator' and retort 'In a while crocodile' suggest that our use of language has evolved around our ambivalence towards separation. It may be that this refers back to the pain of separating from the safety of the womb (Klein 1952) and such phrases serve to ameliorate the pain of the inevitable severance from the mother as we enter into the outside world to become autonomous adults. Indeed the word goodbye is a contraction of 'God be with ye' (*Collins English Dictionary*) with the implication that it is best not to be alone, but if you are then God will protect you.

Although the death of one member in a relationship creates the ending of that relationship, we have the potential to carry the internalized notion or experience of that person around with us for the rest of our lives (Klein 1957). Similarly, as therapists we believe that a 'good enough' (Winnicott 1971) experience of the therapeutic relationship will stay with the client and become assimilated into their psyche. Kleinian therapists would describe this process as the 'introjection' of the therapist as a good 'object' after Klein's theory of the internalization of the mother in the infant via the early feeding process (Klein 1957).

Inevitably all therapeutic relationships come to an end – or should do. Our aim as counsellors and psychotherapists is not to create dependence but to work through it towards a greater independence. Sometimes, the path to independence may involve a period of time during which the client is able to experience dependence on the therapist. This is parallel with the infant and child's dependence on the parents as part of the process necessary for introjection and ultimate separation (Storr 1979a). The termination process of the therapeutic relationship is an opportunity to explore feelings linked with earlier experiences of separation and loss. Ultimately we say goodbye to the client and unless we use the Cummings and Sayama (1995) model where they aim to support the client through their life cycle, we do not usually expect to see them again.

In psychodynamic terms the ending of the therapy has many meanings. At best we talk about 'therapeutic endings' where the process of the end of the therapy has been a therapeutic experience for the client (Strupp and Binder 1984). We also have a sense of 'bad' or 'unresolved' endings where the client leaves without discussing their plans with the therapist, perhaps acting out feelings that they are unable to express within the relationship. Ideally we aim for planned endings. Just as Brutus fantasizes about the benefits of knowing how the day will end, as therapists we have an idea of what a good ending would look like. We hope that the client will have achieved their aims set at the beginning of the therapy, or that they will leave with a sense of having received what they came for. However, like Brutus, we do not know what the details of the ending will look like in advance. For each individual client the ending of the therapy will have its own particular meaning that is inevitably linked with his or her narrative.

One of the defining differences between working in independent practice and working within an organization such as the NHS is that in independent practice the decision of when to end usually falls solely on the two people in that relationship – the therapist and the client. With the exception of a partner or workplace paying for the therapy where resources may be finite there are none of the time constraints imposed by the NHS or cash-limited voluntary agency. This can have advantages and disadvantages for both client and therapist. Later in this chapter I discuss the benefit of working in a time-sensitive way and also the potential danger of the therapist's fiscal dependence (Budman and Gurman 1988) on the client if working with a long-term model.

Context and contract

When I began to contemplate writing this chapter I was thinking purely about endings in independent practice, but soon came to realize that endings in any kind of counselling or psychotherapy cannot be regarded without reference to the beginning. To begin there is the context of the referral. The client's expectations of the counselling may well be different depending on how they were referred. They may arrive by referral from a colleague of the counsellor, by their GP or by self-referral. Usually in independent practice it is the client who makes the initial contact with the counsellor, even if at the recommendation of another professional.

When working in an agency the counsellor can give guidance to the referrer on how to suggest that their client see a counsellor and how to explain what they might expect. Referrals in independent practice, however, are more likely to be from clients who have a range of differing expectations of what counselling is all about. Self-referrers may have heard about psychotherapy on the radio, a friend might have recommended it, or they may have read about it in a magazine or newspaper.

I have had several clients arrive saying that their GP had recommended that they come to see me for a 'chat'. While this may have been what was suggested or what the client had interpreted the GP to have said, the idea of having a chat may feel less threatening than their fantasy of what visiting a therapist would be like. Although I explain that embarking on a course of therapy would involve more than the implied social chat, I also try to empathize with their feelings of anxiety about the prospect of having therapy.

Referrals may come from a variety of sources: via a GP, health visitor, complementary health practitioner (as discussed in Robert Withers' Chapter 7), or a religious leader, to name but a few. Depending on where the counsellor works, this will have implications on the therapeutic work. Particularly if the counsellor rents a private consulting room in the same clinic as the referrer, for example, the client may wonder about whether or not their case is discussed by the health practitioner and counsellor. Therefore, any shared care policies within the clinic need to be clearly spelled out to the client from the beginning. This will also have implications regarding the ending of the therapeutic work. For example, a decision will need to be made as to whether or not the client is referred back to the practitioner and indeed whether or not the client wants the practitioner to know when the work with the counsellor comes to an end.

The way a therapeutic relationship ends is influenced by the way it begins. Because of this it becomes part of the boundary setting. It is important for the client to have a sense of how long the therapy may take in general terms; that whether it is to be short term – 6 to 12 sessions – or open ended – 2–7 years in my experience. This helps to make the client feel safe enough to explore the material that is troubling them and to enable unconscious material to emerge. Therefore the initial contract made by counsellor and client needs to include discussion about the client's expectation of how long the therapeutic process will take and how they will know when they have achieved their aims in that process. If appropriate, there should also be a discussion about their previous experience of counselling and how that ended. This will give the therapist and client a means of exploring what the client found useful or not in their previous relationship with the therapist. It also gives the therapist some idea of how the client may try to re-create a similar dynamic in the new therapeutic relationship (Levensen 1995).

One of the advantages of working in independent practice is that the client and therapist decide together the length of the therapeutic contract. There is the luxury of being able to work in a truly time-sensitive way, whether it be short term or open ended, and where the process may be jointly reviewed as necessary. This is not to say that time can be wasted because of the lack of any time constraints but that the client has a choice about how much or how little therapy they have. Similarly the therapist can make good professional judgements about how much they think the client needs; whether it is short term or more open ended. The final decision can be a joint one created out of the therapeutic relationship.

Endings within the process

Each individual session has a beginning and an end. It is this that contributes to the boundary between the therapist and client. There is a clearly defined time limit during which the client has the whole attention of the counsellor and a safe enough place to explore their material. Any blurring of this boundary (by the therapist being late or changing session times too often) may create uncertainty and a sense of lack of safety. Some clients find it hard to end each session and rely totally on the therapist reminding them that it is time to end. Some will begin to talk about something very painful just five minutes before the end and attempt to continue talking all the way to the door, so making ending the session doubly difficult. This may be a way of avoiding the difficult issues during the session proper and also an unconscious means of attempting to seduce the therapist into giving them more time. Threshold remarks, those uttered just as the client leaves, also tell us about unconscious feelings the client may have towards the therapist. One client I had would often say at the end of the session 'Thanks, anyway.' On exploration we came to realize that he would say this at the end of sessions where he felt that he was disappointed. Because he was a 'polite' man he felt that he had to say something positive even though he could now see that this comment was barbed with his unconscious anger. When a client is paying for the service these remarks take on a more profound meaning.

In independent practice the manner in which the client pays also has a meaning in relation to the end of the session. Often clients have reached the end of the session only to begin writing out the cheque and snatching a few more elicit minutes of contact. Others pay cash at the end, pulling out a great wad of notes from which they pass the few due to me. A hypothesis made by the therapist may be that the client is saying 'Really I am successful out there, I have plenty, I have more money than you therefore I am more potent and don't really need you.' This unconscious communication is material that can be noted by the counsellor and used therapeutically during subsequent sessions. Similarly, threshold remarks, are important to hold on to for the following session. They are spoken in an unguarded moment, possibly to stave off the ending and separation, to defend against the pain of the ending, or indeed as an expression of anger at having to leave. If working psychodynamically, the counsellor is unlikely to respond other than to suggest that this be discussed further next time.

Therapist's illness

When either the client or the therapist is ill the therapeutic work is punctuated with a break. This is so whether or not in independent practice. However, while working independently it is perhaps less likely that the therapist will take time off due to illness. There is no sick pay to cover the therapist when he or she is ill and the temptation may be to take various remedies in order to safeguard their income. One of the many possible communications to the client is that the therapist is omnipotent, or at the very least a martyr and that the client is feeble because they cancelled last week when they were ill.

There is a fine balance between maintaining the therapeutic contract by being there for the client every session and sensibly looking after oneself in order to be available to them next time. I had one client who was experiencing a particularly painful phase in her therapy. As I had a heavy cold I decided to cancel my other clients for that day but not to cancel my session with this particular client. At the beginning of the session this client seemed grateful that I had managed to see her, but she commented on my not looking well. However, as the session progressed she became increasingly angry as we explored how she felt that I was patronizing her by working when I was obviously unwell. She agreed that although it would have been difficult for her not to have the session, she would have managed. I had fallen into the trap of overprotecting her as her mother had when she was an adolescent, as well as being seduced by my omnipotent fantasies of being indispensable.

By its very nature illness is unplanned and if we have to cancel sessions we create an unexpected temporary ending in the therapeutic process. However, it can prove useful therapeutically.

If the therapist has to cancel sessions due to illness the client may well feel abandoned and angry. They may have fantasies about the mortality of the therapist. Alternatively the client may have fantasies of being too much for the therapist and therefore the cause of their illness. These phenomena can be explored later when the therapist is well again.

Although it is common sense, the therapist also needs to think about the possibility of contagion if they are ill; either literally being contagious and passing on their germs, or acknowledging that the client may have fantasies about catching something from the sick therapist. Although this may make them feel more connected with the therapist, conversely it may make them fearful and distrustful.

Particularly in independent practice it is the therapist who has to make contact with the client in order to cancel the session if they are ill, whereas in a GP practice or other agency a receptionist may undertake this task. Speaking directly with a client to cancel a session can accentuate the vulnerability of the therapist whether they have a hoarse voice, or they sound weak with fatigue. Although this may feel like a difficult task for the therapist, the fantasies it creates for the client provide helpful material to work on later. For example, immediately following my summer holiday one year I had food poisoning made complicated by my also being pregnant. I had to take a further three weeks off work to recover. For one very dependent client this was very frightening. He fantasized that I did not want to return to work to see him because he thought that I found him overwhelming. His parents had found his binge eating behaviour overwhelming when he was an adolescent to such an extent that they insisted he leave home.

Interim therapeutic cover

With more serious or long-term illness the therapist needs to consider alternative support for those clients who would find a longer break particularly difficult. Giving the client the option of seeing somebody else and offering a telephone number of a colleague willing to see the client for the interim period may be appropriate.

When asking a colleague to step in it is important to make it clear with them whether it is a temporary arrangement or not as this will affect the way they work with the client. I had the unfortunate experience of a colleague inadvertently taking over one client with whom I had been working for two years while I was on three months maternity leave. My colleague had not really thought through the implications of working on a temporary basis with somebody else's client. The client, furious with me for leaving her, developed an idealized transference relationship with my colleague and decided that she wanted to stay with her rather than continue to work with me when I returned from maternity leave. My colleague agreed that this was possible provided that she discuss it with me first. By the time that she came back to see me the client was adamant that she did not want to come back to complete her work with me but wanted to come and tell me so. My colleague lived nearer to her, was older than me (and perhaps therefore more experienced), but when I suggested that she was still feeling angry with me for abandoning her she could not see this. My colleague had unwittingly colluded with the client's unconscious rage and offered her an escape. Unfortunately, but perhaps unsurprisingly, the client then decided to leave therapy altogether. I was able to discuss this event with my colleague and we agreed that we had both made mistakes. Mine was in assuming that she was clear that the work was to be on a temporary basis, supporting the client to acknowledge her feelings about my abandoning her, while not taking on full therapeutic responsibility. My colleague's mistake was to give the client the ultimate decision about whether she would return to me or not. In most situations this is appropriate; it is the client's decision. However, the difference here is that we had previously covered a lot of ground working on her feelings about me leaving her, acknowledging that it wasn't forever and that I would be back. I was not going to repeat her early experience of being emotionally abandoned by her depressed mother.

Client's illness

Unlike working within an agency, in independent practice when the client takes time off due to illness there is the issue of payment for missed sessions to be addressed. It is important for the therapist to be very clear about their policy on this at the contracting stage so that they feel confident about discussing it with the client if they have 'forgotten' later on. Some clients experience having to pay when they are ill as punitive and no amount of explaining about protecting their space or paying the therapist for being there will make any difference. Containing their anger is important in itself.

Exploration of the meaning and symbolism (McDougall 1989) of the client's illness is also therapeutic. Is it an avoidance of something going on in the therapy, or a reaction to another stressful situation in their lives? Did they telephone to let the therapist know, and if not what are their fantasies about what he or she thought about them not turning up? It would also be appropriate to explore the client's early experience of illness. Did they feel cared for when they were ill or were they left alone to suffer? How this relates to the way they manage their own illness now would be useful to explore. Similarly, how they might have experienced other family member's illness may also be relevant. One client described how her mother would spend weeks lying prostrate on the couch when she was around the age of nine. The client had to learn to cook and care for her younger siblings from this age onwards. She learned to put others before herself and consequently found it difficult to take time off if she was ill. She also felt extremely angry with me when I had to cancel a session due to my own illness. Whether a client decides to attend or cancel the session if they are ill, they may have phantasies about their potential for contagion and how the therapist may feel about this.

Holidays

The way in which holidays are managed will depend on the initial contract. I have found the need to be clear from the outset about my expectations with regard to whether or not clients will have to pay me when they are on holiday. Some therapists expect clients to take the same holidays as they do, expecting payment for any extra that the client takes. I compromise by suggesting that they can take up to four weeks on top of my holidays but that I expect a minimum of four weeks' notice of this. Most people find this reasonable and it enables me to budget my finances if I know in advance of any forthcoming breaks. Any more than an extra four weeks would not only make it difficult financially for the therapist, but may also collude with the client's ambivalence about making a commitment to the therapy.

Therapists' holidays are another matter. Clients need plenty of notice in order to prepare themselves emotionally for the break so that they are not left feeling suddenly abandoned for an unbearable period of time. I endeavour to give six weeks' notice, having said at the contracting stage that I take time off at Christmas, Easter and summer. The notice period gives space to explore feelings of abandonment and the anger connected with this. There may also be feelings of anxiety – will the therapist return? Alternatively, the client may be relieved to have a break from the intensity of the work. Sometimes relief may be expressed in terms of not having to pay for the therapy. Sometimes this may be interpreted as a defence against feelings of dependence, but nevertheless some compensation for loss of the therapist perhaps. The client may also express envy of the therapist who can afford to take a holiday if they cannot.

In independent practice it may be necessary to make a referral to a colleague for somebody who is likely to find the holiday period too long. I have rarely taken longer than three weeks off at a time for a holiday as I think that this is a relatively manageable amount of time that does not interrupt the therapeutic process too much. In deciding whether to give the client another colleague's telephone number while away involves treading a delicate balance between offering protection for the client (and the therapist's anxiety) and infantalizing them. Whatever the therapist does gives the client a message about how they may be perceived by the therapist.

As part of the lead-up to a holiday break I discuss with the client how they imagine they will feel when I am away and what support they can find for themselves. This is not only helpful for the client but also helps to allay any anxieties that I may have about them while I am away.

Fiscal dependence

Unlike working in an agency the ending of the therapeutic relationship in independent practice is vulnerable to the danger of the fiscal dependency (Budman and Gurman 1988) of the therapist on the client. It may take some weeks before that slot is refilled and consequently a substantial part of the counsellor's income will be lost if the ending arrives unexpectedly. This dependence may make it more difficult for the therapist to recognize when it is time to end, so prolonging the therapy unnecessarily.

I have experienced some anxiety when a client has threatened to end the therapy before the agreed time or before I feel that they are ready to leave. I have found supervision to be a useful way of exploring the meaning of the client's threat to leave. It is important to acknowledge the anxiety about the loss of income without letting it colour the nature of the therapeutic interchange. Ultimately it must be the choice of the client whether they stay or leave. It is the responsibility of the therapist to help the client to understand the meaning of why they may want to leave when they do, whether it is before the time judged to be appropriate by the therapist or not.

By contrast there is also a danger in independent practice of the client forming a particularly dependent relationship on the therapist, who might unconsciously encourage the dependence by failing to make it manifest or encouraging the client to overcome it. As Storr (1979b) points out, this is most likely to happen if the client 'is well-off and settles his accounts promptly'.

Ending induced by therapist's pregnancy

When I was training 20 years ago, psychotherapy training seemed to be a predominantly second career, usually for women once their children had grown up or started full-time education. Many of my female peers were at this point in their lives. Therefore the impact on the therapeutic work of the therapist's pregnancy was not discussed on my training course or in the literature of the time. However, with the growth of counselling and psychotherapy in the UK, as described by Glyn Hudson-Allez in Chapter 2, there has been a gradual expansion of literature, particularly in the psycho-analytic field (Steiner 1993; Imber 1995; Goldberger *et al.* 2003; Whyte 2004). This suggests that counselling and psychotherapy are increasingly first career choices and consequently counsellors and psychotherapists are coming into the profession at a younger age. Because of this, it is important to look at how the issues that the therapist's pregnancy raises affect the therapeutic relationship and the ending of the therapeutic process. This is particularly important for those working in the relative isolation of independent practice.

As I began to write this chapter I was contemplating endings with my own clients. I was nearly ten weeks pregnant and thinking I would soon begin telling my clients that we would have to end our work together. We would then discuss whether or not they wanted to continue when I returned to work after six months maternity leave. Either way there would be some kind of ending process that would take place between us. At the beginning I was holding the secret. Would anyone have guessed and if so would they say anything? Did they notice that I looked paler than usual and could they see the bump? I felt glad that they did not know how sick and tired I felt, or that I felt concerned lest my practice be affected negatively. What were their phantasies as I held this secret? I anticipated the time when I would be able to explore this with them with interest and a measured degree of anxiety.

This was my third pregnancy during my career as a therapist. In my experience this has evoked many different responses in my clients and has created a peculiar type of ending, as I needed to take time off work in order to bond with my baby before returning to work on a more part-time basis.

Each ending was an enforced ending – one forced by my own personal desires and needs overriding those of the client. On a smaller scale similar feelings are aroused when the therapist takes a holiday. These occasions are unfortunate for the client, but perhaps understandable. However, becoming pregnant is an active choice made by the therapist and as such it provides perfect ground for re-enacting the birth of the client's sibling. The first child is not loveable enough; the parents want more. It would also arouse strong feelings of loss for someone who had lost a parent or significant carer at an early age.

The rage and envy expressed by one client during my second pregnancy was ultimately therapeutic for her, albeit painful for me. She described her fantasies of wanting to rip the baby out of me. The client's mother had fostered and adopted several children while the client was still a child herself. Inevitably these children were very needy and demanding and therefore usurped her place in her mother's attention and seeming affection. The client was able to link her feelings of rage towards me and her envy of my baby with the rejection she felt from her mother. Again someone else's child was taking precedence over her and she was being abandoned again. Although this was extremely painful, the client gained a better understanding of her difficulty in forming intimate relationships.

During my first pregnancy I had a male client who experienced it as painful evidence that I was in a sexual relationship with a potent man. This was a challenge to his fantasies of possessing me sexually. While it created a rather brutal ending to these fantasies, it also encouraged an earlier resolution to the Oedipal problem than would have occurred had I not become pregnant.

For another client with teenage children my unannounced pregnancy ran simultaneously with her own unplanned one. It was particularly painful as she contemplated terminating her own pregnancy. This created a dilemma for me, as I knew that I would eventually have to announce my situation, but I didn't want it to affect her own decision-making process. Equally I found it painful being pregnant myself and trying to support another woman reach a decision about whether or not to keep her baby. Had I known that this situation would arise I would not have taken on this client, but working in independent practice in an open-ended way meant that this kind of event could not be foreseen and had to be managed in the best way possible. Eventually this client went ahead with her termination and we continued our work until I went on maternity leave. We explored her ambivalent feelings about the situation and she came back into therapy when I returned to work. She is now pursuing her career and feels that she made the right decision at the time.

I noticed that each pregnancy often created a degree of envy in my clients and this provided rich ground for the therapeutic work. One female client felt envious of my ability to have children. She had a hysterectomy while in her late thirties due to complications after the birth of her second child. She experienced this as a painful loss of her femininity and sexuality. We were able to explore this and help her come to terms with a new phase in her life, which did not exclude her as a sexual woman.

Several clients were able to explore their envy of my actual baby whom they fantasized was going to experience the 'perfect' mothering that they had never had. Part of this work was to dispel the myth of perfection and often to assist the client in their acceptance of their respective mother's imperfections and indeed my own imperfection as a therapist who was going to abandon them – albeit temporarily.

Although I have found these times difficult they have also proved professionally challenging. The announcement of my impending leave taking has served to speed up the therapeutic process. With a clear ending in sight, a certain kind of urgency has prompted several clients to move into a deeper mode of working.

As observed by Lyon-Pages (2004) I also found that the intensified transference had a fundamental impact on hastening the therapeutic process. This has not always been the case, of course, and a few clients have chosen to return to the work after my maternity leave. However, my pregnancy still brought up issues for them that may not have arisen had the situation not arrived. In many ways I am reminded of Casement's (1985) writing on therapeutic mistakes. The pregnancy itself is a kind of 'mistake' in therapeutic terms in that it is the therapist's personal life that impinges on the therapeutic relationship, which is usually a taboo. I feel privileged to have had this experience and have learned a great deal from my clients' willingness to share their feelings with me. It has been a steep learning curve as the impact of becoming pregnant was not something discussed while I was in training.

Moving house or changing work venue

The therapeutic environment usually remains constant when we work in independent practice. Unlike the experience of working in many agencies we have the luxury of using the same room for every session. When the therapist moves house or changes their work venue the client may feel bereft even if they go on seeing the therapist in the new place. The client often perceives the therapist's immediate physical environment as an extension of the therapist and any changes made by the therapist are experienced as a loss. The changes may be as subtle as moving a cushion or changing a chair, but the impact can be great. Indeed, having my hair cut short once had a similar impact. The client may have fantasies about the therapist being different in a new environment, no longer being as supportive perhaps, or preoccupied with their own lives and no longer interested in them. As with the therapist's pregnancy, the therapist's life impacts on the client.

In order to minimize disruption I have tried to give clients as much notice as possible about any moving dates and, as suggested by Syme (2002), I have made sure that estate agent boards have not gone up before I have discussed it with them. This is difficult given the uncertain nature of property buying. However, it is important for the client to have an adequate amount of time to explore the feelings that arise from the move. These and related issues come into my Chapter 8 on working from home.

Transitional objects (Winnicott 1971), objects that have moved from the old room to the new consulting room such as a familiar chair or picture, have proved important when I have moved my therapy room. One client was greatly relieved to see what I considered a rather shabby Indian rug positioned in the new room. We came to understand that for him it was symbolic of my perception of him: that I accepted him as he was; in his words 'scruffy, imperfect, colourful and well travelled!'

Another client expressed extreme anxiety about whether or not he would be able to find the new place. We understood this to stem from his fear of having been abandoned by his mother who left him and his father when he was six years old. His father subsequently moved to a completely new area where the client had no friends. With careful attention the experience of my moving proved to be therapeutic for this client. To a large extent he overcame his paralysing fear of moving house himself. He was able to experience that although physical environments may change people don't necessarily change and that he did not have to lose everything, including me.

Death of the counsellor

Unsurprisingly, counsellors like anyone else do not like to contemplate their own death. Writing a will for most people is something that has to be done as a conscious effort, often with financial advisors or solicitors asserting the importance of forward planning. Therefore, writing a therapeutic will detailing the care for one's clients may seem an alien task. However, in the case of our sudden demise what would we do and how detailed should the plans be? At the very least we do need to inform our family of who to contact. We need to consider whether it is appropriate for them to contact clients directly or whether it should be a colleague or supervisor who does this. They will need to know how to access relevant telephone numbers.

Traynor and Clarkson (1992) suggest appointing a counsellor/psychotherapist executor who is sympathetic to the style of working of the therapist, but who is not too grief stricken by their death. Their task would be to inform the clients as soon as possible, make appropriate referrals to another counsellor and dispose of any client notes or audiotapes kept by the deceased counsellor.

This is all very laudable, but to me it also feels like an omni-potent act on the part of the therapist – planning for the aftermath of one's death as though our clients really are our children. It is one thing to be professional and inform a key person in advance of how to contact clients in the event of one's death, but to have everything planned so carefully down to whom to make referrals seems to me to infantalize the client. Even in death we have to be in control. As therapists and counsellors I wonder if we need to be so perfect and would it really be more helpful and caring to our clients to be so? Would not a compassionate telephone call to each client from a family member or colleague with an invitation to contact a relevant local counselling or psychotherapy organization be adequate? The client then has space and choice about how to move forward without everything being so ordered and unreal. Death is rarely neat and organized by its nature and to present it in this way seems antitherapeutic to me.

Death of a client

As discussed elsewhere in this book, one of the disadvantages of working in independent practice is that unless we set up a support group we are working in very isolated circumstances. Therefore, should we experience the unexpected death of one of our clients we would not have the automatic emotional support that would be in place if we were working within an agency. Decisions such as whether or not to visit a terminally ill client in hospital or whether to attend the funeral would have to be made in isolation or in discussion with a supervisor (Syme 2003). In this situation the therapist is still bound by the rule of confidentiality to the client who has died. Pressure from family members to break this confidentiality may be more great if the therapist is seen and engaged with at the funeral. Wheeler (1996) elaborates more on this subject.

If the client's death was through suicide we may feel a huge burden of responsibility, perhaps greater than if we had the support of immediate colleagues as opposed to working inde-pendently (see Adrian Hemmings' Chapter 5 for more on the impact of suicide). The therapist may feel that the client's suicide was a personal attack on them, as indeed it may be. I have only experienced a client's suicide when working in a mental health agency. The client was not someone that I had been working with therapeutically, but he had been a member of one of my activity groups and I liked him. His death had a huge impact on all the workers in the agency, not just those who were working therapeutically with him, and the effects were long lasting. There was much discussion and soul searching amongst the team, but we supported one another in the grieving process and we were also given support by an independent team facilitator/supervisor. The feelings that we experienced ranged typically from sorrow to rage and a sense of failed responsibility. Had I experienced a suicide in my independent practice, I believe that I would need more than my fortnightly supervision to manage similar feelings, particularly as these feelings would be more intense given the intimate nature of the relationship in that context.

Planned endings – the final goodbye

Whether we are working on a short-term or long-term basis, our ultimate aim is to support our clients to become autonomous and no longer in need of our help. We do aim to have an end to the work, even though there may have been a period of time that dependence was so great, that ending seemed an impossibility, certainly to the client, but perhaps also to the therapist.

With short-term work the ending is very much in the foreground and mentioned at each session by the therapist (Mann 1973) so that the final session does not come as a surprise to the client. With longer term work the ending process may begin by the client suggesting that they feel that they would like to stop. Occasionally I have brought up the subject of ending very gently with clients whom I feel have done a great deal of work, but who are finding the idea of separation difficult.

Depending on the initial contract it is usual for me to have at least four weeks' notice to work on the ending period. However, I usually find that clients identify the desire to end and ask for a three-month period of winding down, sometimes even longer. The advantage of this longer period is that it is possible to do a weaning period where the client goes down to fortnightly and then monthly sessions for the final few. During this time we are able to review the work we have already done, explore the meaning of ending the relationship for the client and how this may link to previous endings they have experienced. Often the experience of leaving home will emerge as a significant memory and may become an indicator of how this new ending might be felt differently. I have noticed that old patterns of behaviour often emerge within the therapeutic relationship towards the end of the therapy, for example, the client arriving late as an expression of their ambivalence towards me. It may be a way of telling me that they do not really need me any more or perhaps a way of defending against the pain of saying goodbye. This is obviously important to identify and reinforces the need for an adequate measure of time for the ending process to take place. Finally, having adequate notice of when a client is leaving aids the independent practitioner in planning their workload. It also helps in terms of managing income.

Conclusion

Underlying my thinking about endings is the fact that in independent practice the therapist is alone in dealing with these issues. Unless prearranged peer discussion/supervision groups with other independent colleagues are set up, the independent practitioner does not have the automatic support and back-up that one would expect if working within an agency, should anything unexpected happen. All decisions regarding the ending and all consequences are solely dependent upon how the individual practitioner manages them. Supervision therefore seems to me to be fundamental as a means of supporting the counsellor or psychotherapist working in independent practice. I certainly find that my experience of supervision continues to play a vital part in my being able to think creatively in general about my clients. This is particularly so as we near the ending of the therapeutic work. It is here that we reach the place that Brutus yearns for; when what was unknown has become clearer. The client leaves having completed the therapeutic experience and developed new resources to help them follow a new path for their onward journey.

References

Bowlby, J. (1978) *Attachment and Loss*, Vol. 3: *Loss*, Harmondsworth: Penguin.
Budman, S. and Gurman, A. (1988) *Theory and Practice of Brief Therapy*, New York: Guilford Press.

Casement, P. (1985) Forms of interactive communication, in P. Casement *On Learning from the Patient*, London: Tavistock.

Cummings, N. and Sayama, M. (1995) *Focused Psychotherapy: A Casebook of Brief, Intermittent Psychotherapy Throughout the Life Cycle*, New York: Brunner/Mazel.

Goldberger, M., Gillman, R., Levinson, N., Notman, M., Seeling, B. and Shaw, R. (2003) On supervising the pregnant psychoanalytic candidate, *Psychoanalytic Quarterly* 72: 439–463.

Imber, R. (1995) The role of the supervisor and the pregnant analyst, *Psycho-analytic Psychology* 12(2): 281–296.

Klein, M. (1952) Concerning the theory of anxiety and guilt, in M. Klein, P. Heimann and J. Riviere (eds) *Developments in Psycho-analysis*, London: Hogarth Press.

—— (1957) *Envy and Gratitude*, London: Tavistock.

Levensen, H. (1995) *Time-Limited Dynamic Psychotherapy*, New York: Basic Books.

Lyon-Pages, I. (2004) The therapist's pregnancy: its impact on the therapeutic process/Impact de la grossesse de la therapeute sur le processus psychotherapeutique, *Psychotherapies* 24(1): 17–23.

Mann, J. (1973) *Time-limited Psychotherapy*, Cambridge, MA: Harvard University Press.

Marris, P. (1974) *Loss and Change*, London: Routledge.

McDougall, J. (1989) *Theatres of the Body. A Psychoanalytic Approach to Psychosomatic Illness*, London: Free Association Books.

Parkes, C. M. (2004) *Bereavement: Studies of Grief in Adult Life*, 3rd edn, Harmondsworth: Penguin.

Shakespeare, W. (1599) *Julius Caesar*, in Alexander text (1975), pp. 969–999, Glasgow: Collins Classics.

Steiner, J. (1993) *Psychic Retreats*, London: New Library of Psycho-analysis.

Storr, A. (1979a) Cure, termination and results, in A. Storr *The Art of Psychotherapy*, London: Secker & Warburg/Heinemann.

—— (1979b) The personality of the psychotherapist, in A. Storr *The Art of Psychotherapy*, London: Secker & Warburg/Heinemann.

Strupp, H. and Binder, J. (1984) *Psychotherapy in a New Key: A Guide to Time-Limited Dynamic Psychotherapy*, New York: Basic Books.

Syme, G. (2002) Working from home: a psychotherapist with long term clients, in J. Clark (ed.) *Freelance Counselling and Psychotherapy. Competition and Collaboration*, Hove and New York: Brunner-Routledge.

—— (2003) Social situations and friendship, in *Dual Relationships in Counselling and Psychotherapy*, London: Sage.

Traynor, B. and Clarkson, P. (1992) What happens if a psychotherapist dies?, *Counselling* 3(1): 23–24.

Whyte, N. (2004) Introduction, *Psychoanalytic-Psychotherapy* 18(1): 5–14.

Wheeler, S. (1996) Facing death with a client: confrontation or collusion, counter transference or compassion, *Psychodynamic Counselling* 2: 167–178.

Winnicott, D. W. (1971) Transitional objects and transitional phenomena, in D. W. Winnicott *Playing and Reality*, London: Tavistock.

Index

Note: page numbers in **bold** refer information contained in boxes and tables, page numbers in *italics* refer to diagrams.